GOD
THERAPY

A 7-Step Guide to
Inner Healing & Deliverance

GOD THERAPY

A 7-Step Guide to
Inner Healing & Deliverance

by
Timothy G. Lane, MA

Most G.G. Publishing Company products are available at special quantity discounts for bulk purchase for sales promotions, premiums, fund-raising, and educational needs. For details, write G.G. Publishing Company, 290 Norwood Avenue, Suite 204, Deal, New Jersey 07723, or telephone 1-877-224-9287.

God Therapy by Timothy G. Lane, M.A.
Published by G.G. Publishing Company
290 Norwood Avenue, Suite 204
Deal, New Jersey
www.ggpublishingcompany.com

All scriptures in this book are taken from the King James Version of the Bible unless otherwise stated.

Scripture quotations marked AMP are from the Amplified Bible. Copyright © 2015 by The Lockman Foundation, La Habra, CA 90631. All rights reserved. Used by permission.

Scripture quotations marked ESV are from the Holy Bible, English Standard Version. Copyright © 2001 by Crossway Bibles, a division of Good News Publishers. Used by permission.

Scripture quotations marked NASB are from the New American Standard Bible, copyright © 1960, 1962, 1963, 1968, 1971, 1972, 1973, 1975, 1977, 1995 by The Lockman Foundation. Used by permission. (www. Lockman.org)

Cover design by Pixel Studio
Visit the author's website at lanehelps.com

ISBN-13: 978-0-9990836-0-4

ISBN-10: 0-9990-8360-0

17 18 19 20 21 — 9 8 7 6 5 4 3 2 1

Printed in the United States of America

TABLE OF CONTENTS

INTRODUCTION

In retrospect, I believe the ministry of inner healing and deliverance is something that has been divinely handed down to me from previous generations. My grandfather and father were anointed pastors who moved in deliverance, and my grandmother was an anointed prayer warrior who believed in the power of God. My dad was a small figured man, but full of the power of God. As a child growing up in the church, there were several occasions where I saw my father boldly casting demons out of people. There was a certain man, in particular, who was twice the size of my dad, into martial arts, and a known warlock in the community. Needless to say, he was full of demons, and people were terrified of him. While on the altar at my church, demons began manifesting through this individual. He became very aggressive and agitated. My father boldly and calmly walked up to this man and reached out his hand to place on his head. This man effortlessly grabbed my father's hand and twisted it around as if he was about to snap his wrist. It didn't take an army of men to jump on this man and subdue him because, with authority in his voice, my dad spoke the name of Jesus and commanded the demon spirits to come out of the man. All of a sudden, it was like this invisible divine force took over, and this demon possessed man released my father's wrist and submitted to his commands.

My grandmother grew up encountering the power of God and seeing people set free from demons by the name of Jesus. I loved going over to her house, sitting across from her, on a white sofa with the plastic still on it, and listening to her stories about supernatural encounters with God and demons. I remember my grandmother telling me a story about a very tall man, with a heavy build, who came to their home after serving in the army. A demonic spirit overtook him, and he violently grabbed one of her young children. This man picked up the child by the legs, held him upside down, and was about to slam him on the ground. My petite five-foot-two-inch grandmother, who was the most kindhearted, loving, soft-spoken person you would ever meet, walked up to this man, who was towering over her, looked him straight in the eye and shouted: "Come out of him, you demon of murder!" Immediately his countenance changed and he put her son down and began to weep.

Like my grandmother, I had my own encounters with demons. I became a believer in Jesus Christ when I was eighteen years old. I was a young zealous Christian with the goal of winning the souls of every single person in my high school. Every day, I walked through the hallway with my Bible telling people about Jesus. It didn't matter if it was in a classroom, the lunchroom, the boys' locker room, or on a recess field. Every day, I fasted until school was over because I was hungry to see someone get set free and accept Christ into their hearts. It was not long after I started witnessing at my school that I began to feel an eerie demonic presence following me through the school. It was evident to me that the evil spirits present in my school were not happy with me sharing the gospel of Jesus Christ. There was an incident where I was in a classroom reading my Bible, and a girl, who I never noticed before, sat right next to me and began to stare at me silently. When I looked back at her, I could see a demonic spirit in her eyes. I could tell it was there to intimidate me.

This didn't stop with school; I would constantly come across people with demon spirits, even on my job. I would look at someone and see demonic spirits in their eyes glaring back at me. You might be thinking that was just my imagination. Not the case at all, there was this one incident where I was at my job, and I knelt down to pick something up. When I stood up, there was this woman standing in front of me with this wicked smile on her face. I looked into her eyes and was terrified at what I saw. The best way I can describe it is that it was like a second set of demonic eyes was glaring back at me. Looking for comfort from the fear I was experiencing, I started singing "Yes, Jesus loves me" because that was the only song I could come up with at the moment. This woman's smile became even more wicked, and she began to mock me by singing the song along with me. As I walked away, she followed me, singing and grinning. These encounters with demonized people happened to me so much that I became terrified of demons. Actually, being terrified was an understatement; I was literally shaking in my boots when it came to the demonic. Not to mention, watching old Hollywood exorcism movies did not help me. I remember the first exorcism movie I watched over at my friend's house. With the lights turned off, in a house that I was in for the first time, while the demonic spirit began to speak through the actor in the movie, my friend's brother started acting like he was being taken over. I would've run out of the house or jumped through a window, but I was frozen in a state of shock. Thank God he snapped out of it and started laughing; but there wasn't a smile anywhere on my face, just horror and a desire to leave immediately.

It seemed like no matter how much I tried to avoid the topic and encounters with demons, they made a regular appearance in my life experience. I recall several times during our Sunday morning services at my church, the power of God would get heavy, and people who had evil spirits would scream, jump up, and try to run out of the church. This occurred almost every Sunday, and it gripped me with so much fear I did not want to go to church anymore. When the topic of demons came up, I told my Christian friends how terrified I was of demons, and never wanted to cast out demons from anyone.

This continued until I grew in my relationship with God and realized who Jesus Christ was inside of me. When I learned my identity in Christ, I became fearless against demons. Demonology, demon possession, casting out demons, or any other topic relating to demons became intriguing and exciting to me. I went from not wanting to hear the word "demon" to wanting to know all about them. I would spend days and nights studying about evil spirits and watching videos of people casting out demons. I had no idea that God had a special call on my life to minister inner healing and deliverance. All I knew was that the fear that once gripped me had been transformed into an unusual passion, hunger, fascination with demons and seeing people get delivered from them.

I grew up not believing that Christians could be demonized. Having been raised in a strict holiness church, I was under the impression that the minute you receive Christ, all your issues were resolved and wounds were healed. Only "sinners" had issues and demons. Within a few years of being saved, I recognized and was puzzled that I struggled with major depression. For several days throughout the week, I would not eat. I felt worthless, lacked the motivation to do normal tasks, and would verbally attack myself. At that time, I was a drummer at my church, and our church was known as the "shouting" church because the members would literally praise God for hours while we played "shouting music." There were many occasions where the members were doing what we call "shouting," and I would be playing on the drums crying, not because I was being touched by God's power, but because I was depressed and hurting on the inside. I was very perplexed because, for some reason unknown to me, the more the people rejoiced about Jesus, the more I felt deep depression and uncontrollable sadness, and could not stop myself from crying. No one noticed there was something wrong with me; I guess they figured I was crying because of God's presence. Sometimes on the way home from church service, I would begin to cry and not understand the reason I was crying. There were times where I begged God to kill me because I didn't want to live anymore, but I didn't have a reason for feeling this way. I just knew I carried this overwhelming feeling that I didn't want to feel and "wasn't supposed to feel as a saint." The only way out, to me, was for God to kill me. Even though my father was the pastor of the church, I never spoke to him or anyone about my thoughts of depression and suicide. I learned how to cover up my pain because I felt like the church members would belittle me, tell me I was weak, or say I was not saved because "Christians aren't depressed."

It got to the point where I began to commit what I call *spiritual suicide*. I stopped my normal habit of seeking God through prayer, reading my Bible, and worshipping, and just went through the motions. I began to hear voices telling me things like "God doesn't love you, your parents don't love you . . . nobody loves you." The more I listened to these voices, the stronger and louder they became. Then I began to say it out loud, "Nobody loves me, I'm stupid, I'm a failure, I'm ugly." I was literally tormented by the feeling that I was nothing, useless, flawed and a complete failure. I felt there was no hope for me to be anything in life and in God. My low self-esteem was so severe that I could not look people in their eyes, and I became very isolated. I could not even look at myself in the mirror. I also struggled with sin in my life, which caused me to walk in guilt, shame, and condemnation. There were many days where I cried myself to sleep and wished I would not wake up the next morning. When I woke up, I would just lie in the bed because I had no motivation or energy to get up and do anything. This went on for about four years.

The turning point happened when I was lying in my bed feeling extremely depressed (as usual), wishing I could die. As I was dozing off to sleep, I suddenly and unexpectedly heard the audible voice of God saying, "There is a war going on and you better fight!" I realized that the Holy Spirit was communicating to me that if I decided not to fight, pray, seek God, and resist the devil, the devil was going to take complete control of my life and destroy me. That is when I began to take action, according to Matthew 11:12, which says *"The kingdom of heaven suffereth violence, and the violent take it by force."* I began to seek God, accept God's love and mercy, change my confession, and fight. I started praying until I would pray in tongues for hours a day. Praying for hours turned into me spending the night on the floor because, instead of crying myself to sleep, I would pray myself to sleep every night. I began fasting two to three days a week and spent hours a day reading my Bible. There was a particular time I was on a two-day fast. While lying on the floor in my room crying out to God for deliverance and recommitting my life to Him, I began to choke, cough, and spit up saliva. I had no idea that what was actually happening was my deliverance from a demon of depression and suicide. What I did know is that from that point on, that heavy depression I experienced daily was totally gone. From that moment, many dreams and visions about me casting demons out of people started pouring in, and I would wake up with feelings of God's healing power all over my body.

Despite these encounters with the Lord, I still did not believe that Christians could be demonized. However, there was something in me that caused me to continue my research about the supernatural phenomenon of demons and demonic possession. I read books and studied people like A.A. Allen, Derick Prince, Charles H. Kraft, and Bob Larson, but never accepted that Christians could be demonized. It was not until over ten years after I accepted Christ that I began believing Christians could have demons. It all started because of a conversation, or should I say confrontation, that I would have with a Christian that I was close to. She would try to explain to me how Christians could have demons, and I thought it was my duty to defend the truth of the gospel. I vehemently refuted her claims and was offended that she would even state such an abominable thing. Besides, she'd only been saved for four years and I had a whopping ten years of being a devout Christian. All my life I was taught that Christians could not have demons, and I wouldn't dare allow her to deceive me. Once she realized how stubborn I was, she stopped arguing with me and told God, "You're going to have to show him yourself, and it probably needs to be someone close to him." She had no idea she would be the one God would use for this awesome task. Less than a year later we decided to go to a deliverance service at a conference we were attending. I was overjoyed because, for the first time, I was at a seminar about how to cast out devils—so I thought. As I sat there on the edge of my seat with enthusiasm, in a venue with about two hundred people, something really strange caught my attention. There were ministry workers in the back with rolls of paper towels all over the floor, earnestly ripping off hundreds of sheets and then passing them out to people in the congregation. I figured this was for the "sinners" that we were going to practice on after the teaching. This made me more excited and I couldn't wait. My first official "deliverance service!" I was intensely scrutinizing everything that was going on. I felt like a kid in a candy shop. I had watched deliverance services, read about them, dreamed about them, and now I was a part of one! Then I became confused. These workers were passing those sheets of paper towels to every single person in that room. I was thinking, "Surely I'm not the only Christian present in this service." Then one of the workers came to me and handed me a paper towel. I politely passed it to the person next to me so she could pass it to the person next to us. I then confidently signaled to the lady that I wouldn't be needing any of those towels, which I figured was for the purpose of catching the saliva as the "sinners" coughed up demons. She then gave me this look, almost like she was unconvinced that I didn't need one, and handed me more paper towels, for myself. After about fifteen minutes of teaching on demons, we got to the part I love. It was time to cast out some devils! The facilitator had us say this deliverance prayer, which I did not know why we Christians had to say it because, in my mind, Christians are already saved and delivered. As we began to say this prayer, people began manifesting demons. Four rows across from me I would hear someone cry out. Then in the back somewhere someone would scream and fall out. All of a sudden, like popcorn popping, people all over began screaming and coughing. I looked over at my friend to see if she was enjoying the show just as much as I was, and her eyes got really wide, almost like they were about to pop out. I paid it no attention; maybe what we ate earlier didn't sit well with her. Then, this Holy Ghost filled believer, who I personally knew loved Jesus and was living for Him, held her stomach as if something was turning on the inside. If only you could have seen the look on my face. Then, suddenly, she flopped down right across my lap and began screaming. I shockingly pushed my chair back as if a spider had just fallen out the sky and landed on me. She then collapsed to the floor, screaming even louder. There is no word in the dictionary to describe what I was feeling. That same worker that gave us the paper towels had me move totally out of the way as they commanded demon spirits to leave her. For the first time in my life, even though I was a pastor and new my bible from Genesis to Revelations, I felt like I had no idea what to do. After the service, I was numb and in limbo for the rest of the day and walked around in a daze. For the first time, I thought it might be possible that Christians could be demonized. Days after the incident, she mentioned that she felt she needed more deliverance and wanted me to pray for her. I still felt awkward about it and I reluctantly said okay. As we sat across from each other, I searched the Internet and found a deliverance prayer that I could have her repeat. This is a prayer I saw a minister do online so I figured if it worked for them then maybe it'll work for me. The first sentence said something like, "I am redeemed by the blood of Jesus Christ." I said it and told her to repeat it, but, to my astonishment, she couldn't make it through the first sentence. As she would try to speak, something was stopping her. She would open her mouth as if she was straining and nothing would come out. I thought to myself, "Could this be another demon spirit?" So I said, "In the name of Jesus, you evil spirit, I command you to allow her to speak." To my surprise, once I said that, she was able to finish the sentence. This was only the beginning. As we began to go through the prayer that removed legal rights, broke generational curses, and commanded demons to come out, all of a sudden her voice changed and another voice that wasn't hers spoke and said "I hate you. You're stupid." At first I felt fear, but all of a sudden, this holy passionate boldness came over me. I began to command every demonic spirit that was in her to come out in the name of Jesus and that's exactly what began to happen. One after another, demon spirits manifested through screaming, shaking, crying, and verbally attacking me. There was one point where the spirit in her caused her to jump up and attempt to run away. Even though these demon spirits were defiant, I realized they were subject to my every command. I would speak boldly in the name of Jesus and command the spirits to lower their voices, name themselves, and come out. They tried to put up a fight, but eventually, as I was persistent, they did exactly what I said. For at least four hours, I cast at least seventeen spirits out of her. That was only the beginning! For the next two days we met and I continued to cast demons out of her.

After that incident, I did what I was raised in the church to do: search the scriptures to see if there was any biblical proof of what I just experienced. I then realized there was a biblical backing to substantiate how Christians cannot be possessed (under total control) but can be demonized (areas in our heart, mind, or body that are occupied by demons). Paul the Apostle admitted in 2 Corinthians 12:7 that he had a *"thorn in his flesh,"* which was a *"messenger of Satan."* In this scripture, Paul the Apostle is clearly communicating that he had a demonic spirit and sought God for deliverance. In Ephesians 4:7, Paul instructs the Ephesian church to *"neither give place to the devil."* The Greek word for place means foothold, occupancy, or residence. This scripture lets us know that, as Christians, there are things we can do that can open the door for demonic spirits to come in.

Things began to make sense to me now; it was like pieces of a puzzle started to come together. I started to think about some members I was pastoring who were struggling with various things, and no matter how much I prayed over them and counseled them, they couldn't get set free. Or they would be free for a moment and end up right back in that emotional, mental, and spiritual bondage.

During this time, I was a secular therapist for about five years, and my schooling and training taught me that there is no cure for mental disorders. As a therapist, we were taught to partner with the clients and assist them with managing their disorder. If they couldn't, we had to refer them to get medication so they could be what I call *dysfunctionally functional.* Now I understood why for some disorders, there is no natural cure because part of the problem is spiritual. As I began to ponder my newfound revelation, I felt the Lord leading me to start my own Christian counseling practice which would be focused on inner healing and deliverance. I felt this was the missing component to bringing people freedom. The practice was focused on healing inner wounds and helping Christians remove the places where the devil was occupying their lives. To my surprise, when I began the deliverance part, Christians started manifesting demonic spirits, and demons began coming out through my command in Jesus's name. From lay members to pastors, people came to me and received miraculous deliverance, not only from their inner wounds, but also from demonic spirits. It got to the point where I was doing inner healing and deliverance two to three times per week.

Since then, I have committed my life to studying and practicing inner healing and deliverance. I have seen many individuals set free and delivered. In many cases, I have seen the power of God on full display to heal people's wounds. I have preached at revivals, I have had prayer meetings and prayer lines where people were touched by the presence of God, but I have never encountered the power of God at the level that I have encountered God during my sessions. My clients and I felt the tangible presence of the Holy Spirit in ways we have never felt Him before.

There was a case where I asked a woman to close her eyes and picture Jesus, and she had an open vision of Jesus Christ. As she began to explain what Jesus was doing and what she was seeing, her heart began to beat faster, her breathing escalated, and tears started running down her eyes as she reached her hands out in front of her as if she was literally touching Him. I have seen people totally delivered from clinically diagnosed disorders such as major depression and anxiety disorders. Not only that, but I have also witnessed Christians receive freedom from tormenting spirits and spirits of infirmity that caused them to live a life of pain for many years. There was this missionary who was in constant pain for at least five years because of an incident. During the session, we came against the spirit of infirmity, I commanded the demon to go, and the pain totally left.

My all-time favorite case is with a person I am going to call "Sarah," who was in her early twenties and dealing with depression. Her depression was so severe that it had literally crippled her from doing anything in life. She had dreams and goals, but no motivation to accomplish them. I spoke with her mother, and she told me that she was concerned that her daughter was suicidal. As we went through the inner healing process, you could see by Sarah's expression that her inner pain was being removed and God's power was transforming her. During the deliverance, many spirits came out of her. We then invited the Holy Spirit to fill her up and fill every place where the enemy occupied. As we began to pray, she began what we call "laughing in the Spirit." Then the ministry helper began laughing in the Spirit, and then I began laughing in the Spirit. I then realized that God was taking her depression and replacing it with His joy. It reminded me of Psalms 30:11, which says, *"Thou hast turned for me my mourning into dancing: thou hast put off my sackcloth, and girded me with gladness."* The more we continued to pray for her, the more God increased her joy, and before I knew it, she fell out on the floor laughing in the Spirit with so much joy and peace. After that session, this woman joined our congregation and got involved in ministry, and God is using her mightily. She went from a stagnant, depressed, inactive member to an anointed, loving, happy, and faithful member that contributes so much to the ministry and has the most illuminating smile you will ever see. Months later, I questioned her about the depression, and she told me that she is totally free!

As a professional counselor, I believe inner healing and deliverance is similar to counseling in that it addresses wounds, trauma, and cognitive distortions. Inner healing and deliverance also provide people with practical tools and the support they need to increase their quality of life, maintain their freedom, and live productive lives. As a secular clinician and Christian therapist, I realized that most secular counseling theories teach there is no cure for an individual's condition. I was taught that my goal was to help individuals become self-aware, understand their triggers, develop coping skills, and have a support system. Once this was accomplished, my job was complete, and I could close their case. With severe disorders, I was to provide clinical service along with referring them to a psychiatrist who would prescribe the proper psychotropic medication. However, I believe God has shown me another method that clinicians and believers can add to their expertise when assisting those that have mental and counseling needs.

The God Therapy method described in this book is a combination of therapeutic concepts with biblical principles and invites Jesus Christ to manifest Himself in a way that will bring total healing and deliverance to the person in need. Psalms 103:2-3 states, *"Bless the Lord, O my soul, and forget not all his benefits: Who forgiveth all thine iniquities; who healeth all thy diseases."* When it mentions healing of diseases, this is not just physical but also mental and emotional issues that are having an adverse impact on a person's life. I've seen marriages improve because of inner healing and deliverance. I have witnessed people receiving divine clarity and direction through inner healing and deliverance. I've witnessed people's relationship with God and others improve greatly because of inner healing and deliverance. I've seen people healed from childhood wounds and issues they thought they would carry for the rest of their lives. The exciting thing about the method is that it is a Holy Spirit led counseling, and you never know what God is going to do or what the person is going to experience. Even though the method and process are the same, every session is unique because of the ways Jesus Christ manifests Himself to different people.

Even though secular counseling experience is not a requirement for this model, my clinical experience as a therapist has given me a greater ability to discern issues, disorders, and spirits. It has also given me evidence-based tools that I can use and integrate into the sessions. In my professional opinion, secular counseling and deliverance complement each other because each has a missing component the other needs. I believe a significant number of psychological disorders and issues have a spiritual element that's influenced or controlled by the demonic. Clinical interventions address emotional wounds and distorted thinking, but do not deal with the demons that are usually connected to the problem. On the other hand, people who do deliverance usually do not deal with the inner wounds that caused the demons to gain access. God Therapy brings the two together and addresses both components.

What really launched me into doing inner healing and deliverance and actually starting a Christian counseling practice was a secular client, a little girl, who I will call "Ann." During one of my sessions, she expressed to me that her phobia of dark places was connected to her actually seeing dead bodies whenever the lights were turned off. This was due to a traumatic event she witnessed where she saw the deceased body of someone close to her. This precious little girl was so tormented that she became afraid to close her eyes, and my heart was filled with compassion. I could have gone through the long process of exposure therapy and helping her become desensitized to her experience through having her talk through the trauma or write a narrative explaining her encounter. But I decided to take a Holy Ghost shortcut. Long story short, I prayed for her and discretely addressed those tormenting spirits. She was immediately delivered, and every time she saw me, she gave me the biggest, brightest smile, and tightest hug, and would say, "I can sleep now. I don't see that stuff anymore!"

This book/manual is filled with everything I have learned in the study of inner healing and deliverance theory, as well as the results of years of practical experience my team and I have received by ministering inner healing and deliverance. As you read and utilize this manual, you will gain the concepts and the tools needed to receive inner healing and deliverance, as well as tips and guidelines for doing it yourself. I pray God's blessings to you as you embark on this journey of inner healing and deliverance. So many people in the body of Christ are doing church work but not Kingdom work. Through fulfilling the commission Jesus Christ has given to every believer in Matthew 10:8, the power to *"heal the sick . . . cast out devils,"* not only will your heart be rewarded by seeing lives transformed, but you will also receive a heavenly reward.

CHAPTER 1

WHAT IS GOD THERAPY?

Clinically speaking, God Therapy is strength-based, solution-focused, short-term counseling mixed with some components of cognitive behavioral therapy. God Therapy is strategically structured to get to the root cause of your issue, which requires you to be open about your past and confess your present shortcomings. Inner wounds usually surface in negative feelings such as anger, depression, anxiety, fear, and pain. Even though current circumstances can trigger these emotions, they are sometimes connected to something deeper from your past. It could have been something that happened in your childhood or when you were a teenager. You must find the root cause of the wound and pull it up. It's like when I was a kid: My parents had a fenced backyard infested with yellow weeds. I was disgruntled by the fact that out of seven children, I was assigned to get rid of them. However, the adventurer in me was determined to accomplish the mission. I went through the grass and ripped the weeds out of the ground one by one. This literally took me hours. When I was finished, I thought I'd won the battle, until weeks later the weeds were back. I was so frustrated! I had to start all over and would go through the grass again ripping them out of the ground and throwing them over the fence. They would always come back, and I could not figure out why. It was not until I got someone older to tell me that to get rid of weeds, I must pull them up by the root. Similarly, inner wounds are like weeds. You must identify when the seed of the wound was first planted and pull it up by the root. Only then will the wound be healed and not come back. This is the reason people can be ministered to, feel better, or even get demons cast out of them, but weeks later, they'll be back in the same bondage.

Psalms 33:4 states, *"I sought the Lord, and he heard me, and delivered me from all my fears."* In Hebrew, the word *delivered* means "to snatch away or rid." Therefore, deliverance is the process of purging people of demonic influence, torment, oppression, or control. In Mark 16:17, Jesus said the first sign of a believer is to *"cast out devils."* This passage of scripture teaches us that people in the body of Christ need to do deliverance. Yet, most people in the Western religious culture disregard and dispel the idea of Christians having demons. This has caused a great plague of demonization and mental, emotional, and spiritual dysfunction in the Christian church. Demons survive and thrive where they can hide. When Jesus cast out devils, one of the first things the demons would say is, "Leave us alone!" I'm afraid that the church has answered the devil's prayer because most American churches leave demons alone and don't do deliverance. God forbid an actual demon manifests in one of our services. We'll have security guards carry them out because we have no clue what to do, and how dare someone or something disrupt the decorum of our service. One of my first clients told me a story of being in a church service and a demon manifested through an individual on the first row. The way the people of the Most High God ran out of that church, you would've thought someone walked in there and yelled, "Bomb!" I also don't understand how people can call themselves Christian counselors and not do deliverance. Jesus is referred to as the Wonderful Counselor, and one of the main things He was known for was casting demons out of people. A so-called "Christian counselor" that doesn't do deliverance is really a secular counselor in disguise!

Spiritually, God Therapy literally causes you to have an encounter with Jesus, who is the true healer! Just like psychiatrists rely on medication, we rely on Jesus to be the healer that He declared He was in His word. Like Exodus 15:26, which says, *"For I am the LORD that healeth thee."* Through Godly encounters, you will experience revelation, inner healing, deliverance, and breakthrough at levels that could never be experienced through counseling alone. God Therapy is not about telling you about what God is saying and doing; it is about coaching you to a place where you can hear God's voice, feel God's presence, and see God for yourself.

Psalms 147:3 states, *"He healeth the broken in heart, and bindeth up their wounds."* This means that any person, Christian or non-Christian, who has inner wounds or is under demonic oppression, torment, or control needs inner healing and deliverance. Due to the severity of the broken and dysfunctional family structure, increased prevalence of trauma, and most churches not being equipped and trained to address inner wounds, there are an astounding number of people in the body of Christ who need inner healing. The Hebrew meaning of the word *heart* is "the feelings, the will, or the intellect." Therefore, inner healing is the strategic process of repairing or curing damaged emotions, will, or intellect that usually comes from childhood wounds, trauma, or abuse.

In addition, God Therapy has clinical components of cognitive behavioral therapy, which causes you to identify cognitive distortions, challenge those distortions, and commit to changing those misled ideologies about things and replacing them with the truth. When this happens, you will experience lasting freedom and not just temporary relief. This is just like the Bible passage from John 8:32, which says, *"And ye shall know the truth, and the truth shall make you free."*

God Therapy is different from your traditional Christian or clinical approach to counseling because it includes a component that is encounter-driven and Holy Spirit led. Although clinical experience and biblical counseling experience assists a person in this God Therapy model, it's not required. Even though a person's ability to move in the gifts of the Spirit like prophecy, words of knowledge, and revelation is welcomed in this God Therapy model, and many times can be triggered, it is not compulsory. This method of inner healing and deliverance is practical but powerful. There were times when I had sessions where I was not feeling God and could not think of a clinical technique to use, but as I followed the steps, the Holy Spirit took complete control, and the person received an unbelievable breakthrough as I watched and took notes in amazement.

There was a particular woman I will call "Jane," who dealt with deep father wounds and rejection. To cope, she became emotionally numb and dissociated from those painful memories. It was hard for her to connect with Father God because she projected her feelings of rejection and abandonment from her natural father onto her Heavenly Father. As we proceeded to step two of the God Therapy model, the part that walks the person through forgiving from the heart, she put her head down, crossed her hands, and closed up even more. As the pain in her subconscious began to come into her conscious, it was too much for her to bear, and she could not bring herself to forgive. She wanted to, but she said she did not know how to let go of the past. I knew we could not move any further unless Jesus stepped in and took over the session.

This was when I used the technique mentioned later in the book called Holy Spirit Come. As we began to focus our attention on Jesus and tap into His presence, it was like Jesus stepped into the room and took over the entire session. Once I realized what was happening, I let go of the wheel and let Jesus take the driver seat. This individual, who held her head down with arms crossed, barely talked, and showed no emotion, began to lift her hands and raise her head up while encountering God's liberating presence and hearing His comforting voice. Without me saying anything, she began to forgive the person, and as soon as she did, it was like heaven opened up for her. As Jesus was healing the deep wound, this lady began a joyous cycle of weeping and worshipping. I figured I might as well join in since Jesus had stepped in! Weeks after the session, this lady was very grateful and expressed to me that she could not remember the last time she cried. I knew I had nothing to do with it; I just followed certain steps to usher her into the presence of the Healer.

Zechariah 4:6 says, *"Then he answered and spake unto me, saying, This is the word of the LORD unto Zerubbabel, saying, Not by might, nor by power, but by my spirit, saith the LORD of hosts."* This scripture let us know that the breakthrough you need in your life comes from the anointing of the Holy Spirit, and you must learn how to partner with Him. Whether a lay member or a licensed professional counselor, this process will work as long as you have a clear grasp of the techniques and allow the Holy Spirit to control the session. Jesus Christ is not in some place far away looking down on us or sitting around idle as an observer of the sessions; He's right next to us. He is willing and eager to bring us the healing and deliverance He died for on the cross. You don't have to wait on God or beg Him to show up and show out; God is waiting on you to be courageous enough to face your pain, trust His love and power to set you free.

In Exodus 15:26, it says, *"And said, If thou wilt diligently hearken to the voice of the LORD thy God, and wilt do that which is right in his sight, and wilt give ear to his commandments, and keep all his statutes, I will put none of these diseases upon thee, which I have brought upon the Egyptians: for I am the LORD that healeth thee."* According to this scripture, the healing that comes from the Lord is contingent upon us. With this process, you play a vital role in your healing and deliverance. You have to be willing, honest, and open with those areas of pain that we usually suppress, hide, or deny.

As a school therapist, I was always amazed at my students, who, when questioned about their poor academics, would blame the teacher or other students, but never looked at themselves. Once they took responsibility for the part they contributed, they could take ownership of making the necessary changes it took to improve their grades. Sometimes, you cannot control what happens to you, but you can control how you respond. Just like the saying, "Two wrongs don't make a right." When you're sinned against, it does not make it right for you to carry bitterness, hatred, or unforgiveness. I was at a men's healing conference, and the facilitator shared a story about how during a family function, he found out that his brother had molested his daughter. This brother happened to be in the next room and had no idea what was going on. The facilitator said he walked up to the room where his brother was, opened the door with rage and tears filling his eyes, walked up to his brother, fell on his knees, and said, "I forgive you." He said he did not do it for his brother; he did it for himself. He knew that if he did not forgive, he would have carried that rage, hurt, and pain for the rest of his life. For him to get healed, he had to release it to God, and in order to release it, he had to forgive. That does not mean his brother did not have to face the consequences of his actions. What it means is that the facilitator understood that when we let wounds fester, and carry stuff that God instructed us to let go, it just brings us down. That person that violated you can be dead and gone, but the wound will still be alive, eating you up from the inside out. That's why the Bible instructs you to do the following:

Casting all your care upon him; for he careth for you.
~I Peter 5:7

As a child, I can recall during a hot summer, my parents took me to one of my favorite fast food places: Kentucky Fried Chicken. We ate some in the car and had leftovers for later. I'm not sure how this happened, but someone left the leftovers in the car. It wasn't until weeks later that I found them and figured I would pick up where I left off and ate some more. To my surprise, not only was the food spoiled, but there were also maggots all over the chicken. I couldn't understand how the maggots got there, because the only thing that was in the bag was chicken. My curiosity caused me to ask my mother, and she explained to me when things sit too long, not only do they spoil, but they also attract maggots. When you don't deal with the wounds of your past and you allow them to fester, they become infected, and then maggots, which represent demonic spirits, show up and dwell there. These demonic spirits will feed off your wounds, unforgiveness, and distorted dysfunctional thinking.

As human beings, we innately avoid pain. If you burn your hand on a hot stove, your first instinct is to jump back and steer clear of it for relief. Some things happen in our lives that cause emotional and psychological hurt. It could be related to our childhood, past relationships, father wounds, mother wounds, abuse, etc. Just like the hot stove analogy, these experiences can be so vexing that we choose to shun or suppress them. The problem is, when you have been emotionally and mentally wounded, the hurt and harm it causes just won't dissipate. It's like a child who thinks there's a boogeyman in his room and hides under the covers. The fact is, if there were a boogeyman in the room, hiding under the covers wouldn't make the boogeyman leave. This seems funny, but we do it all the time. We hide the things from our past that have hurt us, and expect them to vanish. Well, they don't. As a matter of fact, they do the opposite.

That thing that you don't want to talk about, think about, or face is what causes the most damage and dysfunction in your life. When you cover up physical wounds, without giving them the proper sanitation and care, it causes the wound to become worse and spread. Eventually, you will develop gangrene, and if that's not addressed, you can actually die from infection. Inner wounds have the same impact on us. Untreated wounds become exacerbated, spread, and eventually show up in other areas of your life. Not only will you be a wounded person, but you will also become a wounded spouse, parent, employee and Christian. You will carry those wounds into your family and ministry, and it will affect your destiny. It will spread to your kids and become a generational wound. I've seen this in the lives of many of my clients. I can recall a client that struggled with severe depression. One day, she called me and said, "Pastor, I see it spreading to my two kids."

I've also experienced inner wounds in my life. As a child, I was wounded by verbal abuse. To avoid the pain, I became isolated and introverted. By the time I was thirteen, I had begun to self-medicate by smoking cigarettes, smoking weed, and drinking. (This is what I call a *numbing mechanism*). I was the class clown because I figured if I made people laugh, they'd like me, not realizing that the real problem was I didn't like myself. There was one particular class that I would get kicked out of every day. I didn't understand that I had an unaddressed wound and it was manifesting in other ways. Some believe time heals; however, my wounds were still there, growing and spreading like an infection within me. As I got older, it worsened and went from me not liking myself to me developing self-hatred and becoming verbally abusive toward myself. I would say things to myself like, "you dummy," "you're stupid," "you're ugly," "your nose is too big," "you're too skinny," and "nobody likes you." I became self-conscious, lacked self-efficacy, and began to self-sabotage. It wasn't until adulthood that I realized how severe and crippling the wounds were. I remember getting my first bank job as a teller. I was afraid to speak to people; I wouldn't look customers in the eye and was hypersensitive to anything people said to me. It was like a light bulb came on, and I realized the wounds in my childhood were showing up in my adulthood and they were bigger and stronger than ever. The boogeyman wasn't in my closet or under my bed, he was inside of me, and I carried him everywhere I went.

I had to figure out how to get rid of the depression and low self-esteem. It became apparent to me that for me to be successful in my career, relationships, and ministry, I had to deal with my inner wounds. The thing is, I didn't know how. I grew up in church and knew all the Bible stories. I could quote many scriptures and recite the books of the Bible, but no one taught me anything about inner healing and deliverance. Even though Jesus spent one-third of His ministry casting out devils, I didn't know how to deal with the demons that were tormenting me. Although Psalm 147:3 says, *"He healeth the broken in heart, and bindeth up their wounds."* I couldn't find anyone who could bring healing to my broken heart. I already knew the religious answer they were going to give me was "just fast and pray." Sadly to say, my story is far too common in many churches, but there is a solution. Not only does God Therapy help you find healing from deep-rooted wounds, and deliverance from demonic bondage, but this book also provides you with the tools you need to bring healing and deliverance to those around you. By reading this book, going through inner healing and deliverance yourself and then going through the God Therapy Training Academy, you will be equipped to deal with the vastly growing need of God's people to be healed and delivered. This is not a book that you read and add to your collection. This book is meant to be a tool that you will be able to utilize to minister, not only to yourself but those in your churches, families, and community. Even though I have gone through inner healing and deliverance, I still utilize certain methods to bring deeper levels of healing to myself and maintain my freedom. Life is full of being wounded, but God doesn't want us to carry those wounds. I remember sitting in my office, and I received a hostile phone call which caused me to feel so much hurt that I couldn't study my sermon for Sunday. I immediately left my office and went to the altar of the church that I pastor. All by myself, I lifted my hands and forgave the person, and while picturing Jesus, I said: "God, I give you immediate access to every area of my heart." As I waited, all of a sudden, my mind went back to the traumatic things I'd experienced in the past and how God healed me from crippling pain. Then I heard the voice of God in my mind saying, "I was with you then and I will be with you now. I will take care of it, take care of you and take care of this church." All of a sudden, all the pain I was experiencing left. All the negative thoughts that filled my mind were now filled with the revelation that God loves and will care for me like a father cares for his son. Then tears poured down my eyes, and I began to walk around the sanctuary thanking God for His healing and love. My pain turned into praise. After Jesus was done with me, I went back to my office and finished studying my sermon. I've learned that the best time to address wounds is when they surface. The worst thing you can do is allow wounds to sit. Pain is not actually the problem, but that is the way God has created your body to communicate with you that something is broken and needs to be fixed. In my younger days, I always wanted a BMW. At that time, I was working downtown at a bank, and I was fascinated by all the BMWs I saw. I would just stare at them and picture myself one day driving one. That day finally came. Even though it was used with a lot of miles, I didn't care, my dream came true. I purchased a silver BMW, with a spoiler, a sunroof, nice shiny rims, and a black leather interior. It was gorgeous on the outside, but it didn't take long for me to realize something was wrong on the inside. Not long after purchasing it, while I was driving, I noticed that my check engine light came on. I ignored it and kept driving. Within a matter of days, my engine began to overheat. You would think I'd have known to pull over and immediately get it towed to the mechanic to be fixed. No way, I kept driving. The situation went from bad to worse, and my engine began to smoke, but I still didn't pull over. I figured I'd drive it home and deal with it later. By the time I got it to the mechanic, they told me there was nothing they could do; I drove too long without getting help. They told me I needed to get a new engine and it would cost me fifteen thousand dollars. This is how we drive through life. There are wounds and issues that surface to let us know something is wrong, but we keep driving—but I thank God that we are never beyond fixing.

> *How God anointed Jesus of Nazareth with the Holy*
> *Ghost and with power: who went about doing good,*
> *and healing all that were oppressed of the devil; for*
> *God was with him.*
> *~ Acts 10:38*

Even though Jesus is no longer with us physically, He lives in every believer and has given us the power to bring healing and deliverance. The problem is, most Christians are not trained and equipped to minister healing and deliverance. When my check engine light came on and my engine started overheating, I didn't address the issue because I was clueless when it came to how to fix cars. As a matter of fact, I barely knew how to change a tire. Sadly to say, this is a representation of what's happening in the body of Christ.

> *My people are destroyed for lack of knowledge.*
> *~ Hosea 4:6*

God Therapy is the solution to this problem. God Therapy brings a certain level of self-awareness and spiritual awareness, so you will no longer be ignorant. The knowledge I have developed through the scriptures, pastoring, and doing inner healing and deliverance has given me the knowledge to realize certain spiritual laws cause Christians not to walk in lasting freedom. The God Therapy model causes you to understand those spiritual laws and walks you through the necessary steps to become free from the bondage that comes from violating these laws. For example, Matthew 9:29-30, *"Then touched he their eyes, saying, According to your faith be it unto you. And their eyes were opened."* What we can draw from this scripture is the spiritual law of what you believe you receive or what you accept you become. If you believe the devil's lies about yourself, God, or your situation, he has legal access and influence in that area. You give demons permission to operate in that area of your life that's connected to whatever that belief system is. This allows those demonic spirits to accomplish their mission to kill, steal and destroy that area of your mind, heart, or life. Usually, where there's a wound, there's a lie connected to it that was planted by the devil and accepted by the person. These lies can be about himself, the world, or even God. For that wound to be healed, you have to identify the lie, repent for believing the lie, renounce it, and replace it with the truth.

Here is a brief example of how a ministry session would go; later on in the book, I will explain each model in detail. You will say to the person you are ministering to, "Close your eyes and say, 'Holy Spirit, what are the lies connected to what my father did or what happened to me when I was a child?'" Ask the person what they see, feel, sense, or hear. You can also have them write it down. Then have the person forgive whoever participated in causing the wound.

The next step is to instruct the person to ask the Holy Spirit, "What's the truth you would like to tell me?" Ask the person what they see, feel, or hear, and write it down. The reason we ask the Holy Spirit is that Jesus said the Spirit's duty is the following:

Howbeit when he, the Spirit of truth, is come, he will guide you into all truth: for he shall not speak of himself; but whatsoever he shall hear, that shall he speak: and he will shew you things to come.
He shall glorify me: for he shall receive of mine, and shall shew it unto you.
you. ~ John 16:13-14

This scripture lets us know that the Holy Spirit has a responsibility to reveal truth to us. After that, walk the person through a prayer of repentance, renouncing the lie, making a commitment never to accept the lie and to receive the truth. Once this is done, the legal rights the demons have are broken, and the thoughts that the wound has been feeding off have now been destroyed. Now it's time for them to encounter Jesus. Have them picture Jesus and give all pain, hurt, and dysfunction connected to those lies to Jesus. Ask them what they see, hear, or feel. Now, release the anointing over the person, minister healing to the wounds, and command the demonic spirits that are connected to the wounds and lies to be cast out. Through this model, I've seen individuals have surreal encounters with Jesus Christ and receive amazing breakthroughs!

It is important that you allow the Holy Spirit to facilitate the sessions and you see what God is doing. You also need to discern when the devil is interrupting the process. This is rarely the case, but I had this client that was so demonized that every time she was asked to picture Jesus, she would have these crazy images or pictures coming to her mind. That's what I call *demonic interference*. I then realized she was too demonized and had too many cognitive wounds for that part of the process. So I had to proceed without that until we dealt with the demons and cognitive distortions.

Throughout the session, we want to hear, feel, or see what God is doing. This is done by giving the Holy Spirit space to speak.

We ask the person to ask the Holy Spirit a question, which is what the Bible instructs us to do when we want answers from God. Luke 11:9 says, *"And I say unto you, Ask, and it shall be given you; seek, and ye shall find; knock, and it shall be opened unto you."* James 4:2 says *"Ye have not, because ye ask not."* After inquiring from the Holy Spirit, we then ask the person we are ministering to what they heard, felt, or saw. By doing this, they are literally seeking to hear God's voice. Afterward, we knock on heaven's door by asking Jesus Christ to come and heal. There was a client who, after walking her through a painful moment, I had her ask Jesus, "What do you have for me instead?" She then saw herself as a child; Jesus was with her, and they were playing on the merry-go-round. Then I felt to ask her, "Did your father ever play with you?" She said, "No." I then said, under the guidance of the Holy Spirit, "You've missed your childhood, and Jesus wants you to experience what you missed as a child." She then began to cry. Then I had her go deep into the vision and spend time with Jesus on the merry-go-round and allow herself to be a child again. Those tears turned to joy as she closed her eyes and played in the park with Jesus. You see, we didn't know, but the Holy Spirit knew that was a deep wound and He knew what she needed to experience in order for her to be healed. Inquiry is so important because whether we feel it or not, Jesus is always working. If we don't ask the person what they see, feel, or sense, we'll miss the therapeutic move of God. This method will also show you if demon spirits are working or not. After praying a prayer to break generational curses, I asked a person what they felt, and they felt needles pricking their hands. That's when I knew it was a demonic manifestation and was able to cast out the devil.

Also, when you ask a person, "What do you see, hear, feel, or see?" It places them in a place of seeking or searching for Jesus to show up in the session, and that's usually what happens. There was a client who dealt with severe guilt, shame, and condemnation and felt disconnected from God. As I began to minister to her through the scriptures from step one of the God Therapy model and then led her through the prayer and encounter step, she closed her eyes and began to have a divine encounter with Jesus Christ. She began to encounter that the God she thought was so distant and displeased, was actually near and loving on her in ways that made her state: "I've never felt this before." As she sat there weeping under the power of God, you could feel the room charged with God's presence. As I got to the step where the counselor prays, the Holy Spirit began to give me things to say to her about how much God loves her and how He's not like her natural father. She began to weep even more and began to share how she came "burdened and heavy," but she was now feeling the peace, love, and joy of God. Then her tears of healing and appreciating the love of God turned to laughter. I've had numerous sessions where the time limit of the session elapsed, but the person was still under the power of God and having a deep heavenly encounter.

During the counselee's prayer portion, they are speaking and making declarations because the Bible says we have authority to speak to mountains and tell them to be removed.

For verily I say unto you, That whosoever shall say unto this mountain, Be thou removed, and be thou cast into the sea; and shall not doubt in his heart, but shall believe that those things which he saith shall come to pass; he shall have whatsoever he saith. ~ Mark 11:23

This is a strength-based approach, and it causes the person being ministered to, to literally tap into the power God has given them and release the healing anointing of God into their wound. In a sense, they are ministering to themselves. Once you've mastered this model, you will find that it not only works on others, but it works for you too!

CHAPTER 2

KNOWING GOD'S VOICE

But strong meat belongeth to them that are of full age, even those who by reason of use have their senses exercised to discern both good and evil. ~ Hebrews 5:14

As I stated before, it's important to hear, feel, and see what God is doing. According to this scripture, a mature Christian has to be able to discern both good and evil. The reason being is that everything that we hear, feel, or see is not God. It can be one of three things: you, God, or the devil. Your duty is to discern who is speaking so you can make sure the Holy Spirit is facilitating the sessions, not you, and definitely not demonic spirits.

I don't know about you, but as a young Christian, I always wondered about how to know God's voice and how God speaks. For the prophet Elijah, it was a still small voice. For Daniel and Joseph, it was in dreams and visions. There are many ways and avenues that God speaks; here are the four main ways:

1.   God speaks through impression.

For the prophecy came not in old time by the will of
man: but holy men of God spake as they were moved
by the Holy Ghost.
~ 2 Peter 1:21

But ye have an unction from the Holy One, and ye
know all things.
~ 1 John 2:20

According to the scriptures above, God speaks to us through unction. The Greek word for *unction* means "the anointing," which represents the presence or the pressing of God. There are times when I am preaching a sermon, and I can feel the presence of God while I am about to speak or while I am speaking. There were times when I was in a counseling session, and it's like the Holy Spirit's thoughts are pressing through my thoughts, and I can feel the anointing as I yield to what I feel God is saying. One time, while doing counseling in a school, I was walking in the hallway and overheard a woman complaining about how she had an accident. Her right arm was swollen and in so much pain that she couldn't move it. I didn't hear a voice, but I felt the presence of God on me pressing me to pray for her. I walked over to her, inquired about what was wrong, and asked if I could pray for her. When I laid hands on her arm, I could feel the presence of God moving out of me into her. Within seconds, all the pain was gone, and the swelling immediately vanished. While moving her arms up and down in amazement, she began screaming praises to God.

When you feel God's presence, it's the Holy Ghost giving confirmation and assurance that it is Him. I am not saying you will feel something all the time, but God will direct you through His presence or pressing.

I call this feeling *what God is doing or saying*. If you are ministering in a session, you or the individual will feel something like the peace of God or the love of God. Sometimes, God will allow you to feel what spirit the person is experiencing. This is called discernment. One time, I was ministering inner healing to a woman, and while she was under the power of God weeping with joy, suddenly, I felt lustful. I knew this wasn't something I was struggling with; it was a spirit within her. Almost instinctively, I spoke to the spirit and said: "You spirit of lust, come out of her." When I said that, her body began to jerk and she vomited the spirit up.

2.   God speaks through vision/pictures/dreams.

> *In the year that King Uzziah died, I saw the Lord,*
> *high and exalted, seated on a throne; and the train of*
> *his robe filled the temple.*
> *~ Isaiah 6:1 NIV*

> *Joseph had a dream, and when he told it to his*
> *brothers, they hated him all the more. ~ Genesis 37:5*
> *NIV*

The prophet Isaiah is describing a vision or his mind's eye seeing the Lord. On the other hand, God spoke to Joseph through dreams. God speaks to us through dreams and visions. A dream is something God shows you while you are asleep. A vision is something you see while you are awake. There are various levels of visions. You can have a *light vision*—this is when a picture or an image comes to your mind; or you can have a *full vision*—this is when you're in a trance-like state and you can literally see things in the spirit. I have had several clients who I've asked to picture

Jesus; they would go into full visions and describe in detail what they were seeing and what was happening to them. During the sessions, God will speak either to the person being ministered to or the person doing the ministering. While ministering to this one lady, I saw a picture of her holding a baby. I then realized God was showing me what was in her future.

3.   God speaks through His word.

> *This book of the law shall not depart out of thy mouth; but thou shalt meditate therein day and night, that thou mayest observe to do according to all that is written therein: for then thou shalt make thy way prosperous, and then thou shalt have good success.*
> *~ Joshua 1:8*

> *He sent his word, and healed them, and delivered them from their destructions. ~ Psalms 107:20*

There's an old mother in the church where I pastor that talks about how she dealt with heavy rejection as a young Christian. This was due to her being neglected by her parents growing up, which caused an inner wound of rejection that never healed. The rejection she felt toward her parents transferred into her feeling rejected by God. One day, she was reading her Bible and read Ephesians 1:6 that said: *"He hath made us accepted in the beloved."* She said God spoke to her through this scripture and she was totally healed from a wound she carried for over thirty years!

The Bible is more than just a book. In Romans 1:16, it says that the Bible is the *"power of God unto salvation to every one that believeth."* Therefore, it is imperative that you have a firm knowledge and understanding of the scriptures. You will notice that

I've provided scriptures with each God Therapy step. This is the foundation for healing. Most clients are dealing with inner wounds and demonization because they are out of alignment with the scriptures. For example, Matthew 18:35 instructs us that when we forgive, we must forgive from the heart. A lot of people struggle to forgive, and if they do forgive, most people forgive from their head and not their heart. When you forgive from your head, you disconnect from the pain, which makes it easier to forgive but doesn't address the wound. The problem with this is that the wound never heals and the demonic spirits connected to the wound are never addressed. True healing and deliverance begin when a person forgives from their heart. This brings a person back in alignment with God's word (which tells us to forgive from the heart), destroys any legal ground the devil has, and allows God to release His healing power. This is just one example, but as you allow the word of God to minister to you and you come back into alignment with His word, you will be amazed at how His healing power will penetrate through any pain, distorted ideology, and strong demonic hold.

For the word of God is quick, and powerful, and
sharper than any two-edged sword, piercing even to
the dividing asunder of soul and spirit, and of the
joints and marrow, and is a discerner of the thoughts
and intents of the heart.
~ Hebrews 4:12

There was a client, I'll call Zoe, who was carrying extreme guilt and shame because of past sins. As we walked through the first step of the counseling session, I could see her countenance change. I inquired how she was feeling. She told me that she felt shame and condemnation, which she regularly experienced. I began to share scriptures about God's love and how according to the Scripture, when we repent, He not only forgives, but He also forgets! As the Holy Spirit directed me through scripture, God's word began to pierce through those wounds and spirits of shame and condemnation. Before I could get to the step where she has an encounter with Jesus Christ, Jesus Christ stepped in, and the woman began to weep. I asked her what she was feeling, and she stated that she was feeling the love and fire of God all over her. I was in awe as I sat back and observed as the power of God began to heal those wounds and replace them with His love and assurance of His unconditional love.

Another important point about God speaking through His word is, if it doesn't line up with the word, it's not God.

Beloved, believe not every spirit, but try the spirits whether they are of God: because many false prophets are gone out into the world. ~ 1 John 4:1

There was a woman that was looking for her soul mate and shared with me that she wrote on a sheet of paper what she wanted in a man and asked God to send him. Within a week, "God sent him" because everything that was on that paper, he had it. The only thing was, he was already married. With confidence, I told her "That wasn't God; the devil tricked you." Her mouth dropped. She couldn't believe she was hoodwinked by the devil. Can you guess how I knew that? I'm not telling you the answer.

One of the best ways to test a spirit is through God's Word. It can look good, smell good, seem good, but if it goes against the Word of God, it may be "good," but it's not God. Look at what Paul said to the Galatian church:

But though we, or an angel from heaven, preach any other gospel unto you than that which we have preached unto you, let him be accursed.
~ Galatians 1:8

4.   God speaks thoughts.

I remember right before a service, a mother was sick and asked the saints to pray for her. She was experiencing headaches, dizziness, and fatigue. As I was about to lay hands, I had this thought that she was feeling that way because she didn't eat anything. So before I prayed, I said, "Mother, did you eat anything before you came to church?" She thought for a second and then said: "Oh, I forgot to eat, I was so busy reading the Sunday school lesson." After we had prayed, I took her over to the kitchen, sat her in a nice comfortable chair, and gave her a hot bowl of chicken noodle soup, and she was miraculously healed.

God speaks through our thoughts, but we must be sure it's God. Here is a tip on how you can verify to see if what you hear in your head is you, God, or the devil. If you believe God is telling you something, don't just say "God said," because you could be wrong. A safe way to say it is to put it in the form of a question. Notice I didn't say to the mother, "God said you're sick because you didn't eat." I asked her if she had eaten anything at all that day. That was me testing to see if what I was hearing was me or if it was actually God. Her answer was a confirmation for me to whether it was God or not. We must be very careful when telling people "God said." I was at a church conference, and this woman who I was sitting next to began to tell me, almost brag to me, about how she was a prophet. She began to prophesy to me that God was leading me to leave my church and he was going to put me under a leader that would elevate me. I looked at her and said, "Ma'am, I am the senior pastor at my church." Let's just say her gift immediately left and I could finally enjoy the service without distractions.

Those are just a few ways God speaks. For some people, God speaks to them more in one area than the other. People can be, what I call, hearers, feelers, or seers. A hearer can hear what God is doing, a feeler can feel what God is doing, and a seer can see what God is doing. I am a feeler and a hearer. Usually, while I am ministering, I can hear or feel what God is doing, or my discernment will allow me to feel different spirits a person is experiencing. I've worked with people who are seers, and they can literally see things in their spiritual mind.

Just like with any gift or calling, whether natural or spiritual, experience and practice will assist you in becoming more sharp and clear with knowing God's voice. It's okay if you don't get it right all the time. Just keep at it, and you will grow and get better and better.

CHAPTER 3

CAUSE TO INNER WOUNDS & DEMONIZATION

There are various issues that cause us to have wounds and become oppressed or demonized. I would like to take some time to talk about childhood wounds. About ninety percent of the client's that I've walked through God Therapy had unaddressed childhood wounds. Most of the issues were molestation, verbal and physical abuse and parental neglect. Unfortunately, there are a lot of families who carry family secrets or do not deal with family issues or trauma. Early intervention is the best intervention. The longer an issue sits, the worse it becomes. In addition, whatever issues are not addressed in childhood transfer to adulthood. Secrecy is destroying a lot of our families.

Ephesians 4:26-27
Be ye angry, and sin not: let not the sun go down upon your wrath:
Neither give place to the devil.

What we can gather from this scripture is that when you don't deal with emotional issues such as anger, depression, hurt, fear, etc. and allow them to linger, it opens the door for the demon of that thing to enter you.

As a teenager, I used to go to the bank with my father. Down the stairs was this huge vault that seemed to be a foot thick with large circular handles. Behind that was a steel gate, and behind that were metal boxes. Years later, I became employed at that bank and found out that was the safety deposit box vault. It's an area where people put their belongings that they don't want anyone to see or have access to. This is a perfect picture of what we do with pain. When we experience trauma such as childhood trauma, teenage trauma, or adult pain, we have the propensity to lock it in a storage area deep in our memory, deep in our subconscious. The reason is that we don't want to deal with the pain. Usually, when the pain or trauma occurred, we didn't have the mental or emotional capacity to carry it, so we buried it hoping it would just go away. We don't talk about it or think about it because of the false perception of "out of sight, out of mind." The problem is that the wound doesn't go away—as you get older, it grows, compounds, and even gets stronger. You develop emotional wounds, mental wounds, dysfunctional defense mechanisms, and triggers. These wounds don't stay hidden; they surface in ways you might not be aware of. You may have no idea that your current personal struggle, attitude, mental illness, unhealthy ideologies, or relational challenges are actually connected to that pain. Also, not only is the pain locked in that storage area, but also demons can hide there because demons live and thrive in dark places. There was a client with whom I was doing inner healing, and as we were walking through the God Therapy model, the Holy Spirit took over and traced her pain back to a childhood event. As she recalled that childhood event, she began to picture an inner child behind a big wall. She felt like that wall was protecting her, but the Holy Spirit told her that the wall was actually keeping God out and keeping the pain in. I asked her to say this simple prayer, "Jesus, I give you permission to come behind the wall and heal my wound." Then the Holy Spirit prompted me to tell her to ask Jesus to become her wall. As soon as she said that, a demonic spirit manifested and began to growl. You see, when we bury pain, we're also burying those demonic spirits that are connected to the pain. They are what I call *demonic worms*, that like to hide deep in our dirt. The more we hide our issues or push it down, the deeper those demons can hide. Inner healing allowed me to dig up the pain that was buried and gave Jesus access to the wound, and without me even doing deliverance, that strong demonic spirit manifested because it couldn't resist the light of Jesus Christ that exposes darkness. What I am trying to say is, for true healing to take place in your life, that locked box filled with pain has to be opened.

There are certain steps or keys that need to be utilized in order to unlock deep inner wounds and bring healing. This may seem difficult because the pain is so great, but I have good news for you: God has given us the keys, and even though it may be painful, once you master this model, it won't be difficult!

And I will give unto thee the keys of the kingdom of heaven: and whatsoever thou shalt bind on earth shall be bound in heaven: and whatsoever thou shalt loose on earth shall be loosed in heaven.
~ Matthew 16:19

Once you understand how to use the keys and know which keys to use, you can go deep into wounded areas or memories, release the healing power of God, and kick out whatever shouldn't be there. Part of this also includes addressing any cognitive lies associated with the pain, replacing the polluted thinking patterns with ways of thinking that are constructive and empowering and inviting Jesus to bring healing and deliverance.

Why is it important to verbally invite Jesus? Revelation 3:20: *"Behold, I stand at the door, and knock: if any man hear my voice, and open the door, I will come in to him, and will sup with him, and he with me."* This scripture informs us that Jesus is always eager to come in and minister to our needs, but He has to be invited. He does not come where He is not wanted or invited. When we choose to suppress and not confess our issues, then we fail to welcome Christ in that area.

Through the many sessions of inner healing and deliverance I've done, what I have realized is that the most challenging part is not the wounds or the demons, it's getting the person to cooperate with the process. This is because the process requires you to face the wound or event that we innately avoid, suppress, and hide. Your level of breakthrough is connected to your level of openness. I've had sessions where I was able to go through the entire God Therapy model within two hours, and the individual was totally healed and delivered because of their willingness and openness about their wounds. On the contrary, there were other sessions where it took at least five sessions to bring the deep-level healing the person needed. There was this particular client with whom I was working through the trauma in her life. As I had her close her eyes and dig deep into her past, she saw this little girl within her in a dark room peeping out the door and then shutting the door. I asked her if she wanted to speak to that little girl, and she said no, that she was not ready. That's when I understood she had deep childhood trauma that she wasn't ready to address yet, and that was okay. Sometimes, there are levels and layers of healing and deliverance. If need be, it is important to keep going through inner healing and deliverance until you feel you are totally free.

CHAPTER 4

HEALING THE INNER CHILD

I would like to take more time to talk about the inner child. While digging into those deep, dark places, you will sometimes find that even though you may be an adult, there is an inner child that is still wounded and traumatized. This is not saying that people have dissociative identity disorder, but when we are faced with trauma, severe pain, or abuse, our body has a natural way of disassociating. Things that adversely affect our conscious get buried in our subconscious so we can survive the moment. Your body has a way of self-numbing, but that doesn't mean the wound is not there. What happens is, if that wound is not properly addressed, you can emotionally and mentally get stuck in that moment where the wound occurred. As I stated before, a lot of people aren't aware of this because it is living in their subconscious. Inner healing brings things from the subconscious to the conscious. Having a wounded inner child is a big issue when it comes to sexual abuse. This is a topic where unfortunately our culture hides. If a child is sexually abused, it's crucial that they get the proper care, support, and therapy; if not, that pain will remain. Even though they may bury it, they will still carry it, and as an adult, it will show up in things like their self-esteem, self-motivation, homosexuality, promiscuity, social skills, trust, spirituality, etc. They may explode, that is, become a very angry person that's easily triggered; or implode, meaning they become very reserved, isolated, and have a catatonic disposition. Here are some steps in bringing healing to your inner child:

1.   Identify the inner child.

You can do this by closing your eyes and picturing yourself as a child during the time the trauma or wound occurred. Do a mental narrative of what was happening and how it made you feel. You also can talk out loud or write it down on a piece of paper. As the wounds begin to surface, that's your inner child that's carrying that wound. If your inner child is still wounded, those same feeling will manifest in your adulthood. That inner child may still be afraid, angry, ashamed, vulnerable, etc. It's important to get to know your inner child and what they are going through. My counseling team, which consisted of a group of men, believed that in order to be an effective therapist, you needed to go through it yourself. We would do this by sitting in circles and discussing our issues. I noticed that every time it was my turn to talk, my heart would beat fast, my hands would sweat, and I would become stressed. For years, I ignored this, but I finally decided to trace it back to the root. While looking within myself, I realized that there was a wound that I experienced in my childhood that caused me to be afraid to speak in front of men and I carried a belief system that I was incompetent. This was my inner child who was still wounded by past trauma.

2.   Release the pain that the inner child is carrying.

As you are doing the narrative about the trauma or painful event that wounded your inner child, it's important to allow the pain to surface and to release it. This is done by allowing yourself to cry, be angry, hurt, etc. Take deep breaths and picture yourself releasing the pain as it surfaces. It also helps to make a noise as the pain is surfacing. Also, as you feel the wound, picture Jesus holding your inner child and you releasing all of the pain, hurt, and anger into His loving chest as He cradles you.

3.   Develop a healthy relationship with your inner child.

We tend to do to ourselves what was done to us. If you grew up under verbal abuse, then, as an adult, you can become verbally abusive toward yourself. If you grew up in a strict household, then you can become hard on yourself and have unrealistic expectations for yourself. One of the healthiest relationships you need to have to live a happy life is a loving, supportive relationship with yourself. In order to soothe and relieve difficult emotions from your inner child, you have to be compassionate and loving to yourself. Most of us continue to wound our inner child because of our negative self-talk or unhealthy thoughts we have toward ourselves. When we have a poor relationship with ourselves, we become emotional and mental masochists and continue to wound an already wounded inner child. For example, your inner child might be wounded because you did not receive the love you needed from your parents. Your inner child is carrying rejection. In order to heal that inner child, you have to accept your inner child by loving on yourself and speaking compassionate words to yourself. Tell yourself it is okay to feel hurt and wounded. It doesn't mean you are weak or something is wrong with you, it means you've been hurt. Let your inner child know that even though it was neglected as a child, the adult you is going to care for it, protect it, and love it. Speak to your inner child about the love of Jesus and how He will never leave nor forsake you. In a sense, you have to be the parent to that inner child that you never had. This may sound weird, but clinically and spiritually, it works.

If you were abused as a child in any way, you may be an adult, but there is a wounded child in there that still needs to be loved, comforted, and ministered to. I've had many sessions where I realized that I was no longer talking to the adult person but the inner child. There was a case where an individual was severely wounded because of verbal and physical abuse from both parents. During the session, the person appeared flat and non-emotional. When inquiring about the person's feelings regarding various painful events, the person consistently responded that they had no feelings. This person did not shed one tear. This let me know that the wounds this person experienced were buried deep inside, and they'd coped by numbing themselves. For that person to be healed, I didn't need to talk to the physical person sitting in front of me, but the inner child that was hiding within. I needed to get from their head into their heart. I needed to get from their conscious to their subconscious where the wounds were buried. Without me sharing with the client what I was thinking, I began to go through the seven steps of the God Therapy model, and all of a sudden, I saw a change in the client. This person that was flat and stated they had no feelings had a tear running down their face. Just a side note, even though most of us were erroneously taught not to cry, crying is a way that the body naturally releases pain. As the individual began to cry, I asked what they were feeling, and they stated nothing. This person was so detached and numb from the pain of their past that they were not conscious of what was visibly happening. So, I continued with the process. By step 3 or 4, the person stopped me and said she saw a little girl, in a dark place, behind a closed door, and she was scared. The person then told me that they felt vulnerable. Within myself, I was leaping for joy because I knew a breakthrough was taking place because we were at the root cause of her issue. That inner child, the subconscious part of her, that part of her that disassociated from her present reality for her to have some level of normalcy, was the one that needed to be healed and delivered. As we continued, I began to address the inner child and the wounds she was carrying and invited Jesus Christ to come and heal her broken heart. This person that was guarded and non-emotional began to weep, speak in tongues, and praise God. She got so caught up in God's presence that she forgot all about me and the session. Without me even addressing the demons, she began experiencing deliverance. Demons began to manifest and come out of her.

Almost every time during the God Therapy process, I have experiences where Jesus has completely taken over, and I sit back and follow His lead. A lot of times during the sessions, you and others participating will also encounter supernatural phenomena. My assistant shared with me that while the lady was crying and praising God, she smelled a strong scent of bleach to the point where she could barely stand it. There wasn't any bleach close to the room. I explained to her that she was receiving a word of knowledge that this person was going through deep cleansing. During this God Therapy process, these types of encounters are normal. Even though her healing and deliverance wasn't complete in that first session, because we ran out of time, the process had started. Again, the level of deliverance and the number of sessions you will need depends on how open you are and where you are in your relationship with Jesus Christ and your relationship with yourself.

After reading this book, if you feel like you are in need of inner healing and deliverance, I would love to work with you. You can visit Lanehelps.com to contact my staff or me for ministry. Also, God has not only called us to go through inner healing and deliverance, but He's called us to do it. This book is also a prelude to my God Therapy Training Academy where I get even deeper about inner healing and deliverance and train you in mastering the seven steps of the God Therapy model. Visit my website and contact me for the God Therapy Training Academy and coaching sessions. Going through inner healing and deliverance is a liberating experience, and doing inner healing and deliverance is an exciting and rewarding ministry. There are people all around you—on your job, in your family, and definitely in the church—that need you to step up into this ministry so lives can truly be changed for Jesus Christ. It doesn't matter the size of your church or what your ministry title is or isn't; we are not fulfilling our obligation as Christians if we're not doing inner healing and deliverance.

Heal the sick, cleanse the lepers, raise the dead, cast out devils: freely ye have received, freely give. ~ Matthew 10:8

And these signs shall follow them that believe; In my name shall they cast out devils; they shall speak with new tongues.
~ Mark 16:17

And when he called unto him his twelve disciples, he gave them power against unclean spirits, to cast them out, and to heal all manner of sickness and all manner of disease.
~ Matthew 10:1

We cannot be content with being mediocre Christians. As you continue your journey by reading this book, I pray that your heart would be stirred to learn it, go through it, and then do it.

CHAPTER 5

MINISTRY ASSESSMENTS

The God Therapy inner healing and deliverance process consists of four main stages; I will give you an explanation of the necessity of each:

1. The Pre-Ministry Assessment
2. Spiritual Assessment
3. Maintaining Your Freedom
4. 7-Step Model to Inner Healing & Deliverance (God Therapy)

PRE-MINISTRY ASSESSMENT

God Therapy is not talk therapy, crisis intervention, or a coaching session; it's inner healing and deliverance. This means the person being ministered to needs to identify specific things they need inner healing and deliverance from. This enables the sessions to stay on track, results to be measured, and time not to be wasted with people who are not willing to do the work. When ministering inner healing and deliverance, your objective is not to fix their external problems but work with them to deal with their internal bondage. A lot of times, our external problems are connected to what's going on internally. You only can be as happy on the outside as you are on the inside. You only can be as free on the outside as you are on the inside. Material things like money, cars, houses, and relationships only enhance and illuminate what's happening on the inside. There was an NFL football player who committed murder and suicide. How can a twenty-seven-year-old NFL player, at the peak of his career, who was making $40 million a year, commit murder and then suicide? That's the result of unaddressed inner wounds. It doesn't matter how much money you make, how many friends you have, or how successful you are in your career; unless you deal with your inner wounds, you will never have outer peace. If you're not free internally, you can have these things and still be miserable. Or, these things will give you temporary pleasure while you will still carry long-term pain. Some people blame others for their problems without realizing the real problem lies within. I always tell my counseling group, when you point one finger at somebody else, three fingers are pointing right back at you. The purpose of the pre-ministry assessment is to identify specific emotional, mental, and behavioral issues that need to be healed. Once inner healing and deliverance take place, you will know you've experienced freedom because you will no longer have issues in those areas that the wounds and demons are connected to. When a surgeon is performing surgery, he or she knows exactly what they're removing. In a sense, you are a spiritual surgeon; each session has to be systematic and targeted. Also, there are people who, even though they're dealing with a tumor, may want a Tylenol. What I mean by this is, you just want a temporary fix or just want to feel better but don't want to deal with the root issues and make the necessary changes to be free. In order for inner healing and deliverance to be effective, you have to be willing to go on an inward journey with Jesus by digging deep within yourself, facing the hurt, and doing whatever it takes to be healed. If not, inner healing and deliverance will be a waste of time. Just like if a doctor tells a person their sickness is connected to unhealthy eating and they leave the doctor's office feeling better but go to an all-you-can-eat fried chicken and rib restaurant.

The pre-ministry assessment identifies three things: The external symptoms you're dealing with, what wounds you may have, and what you need inner healing and deliverance from (view Appendix A). This also gives the person ministering inner healing and deliverance an opportunity to pray for you regarding specific things and hear what God may have to say before the session even starts. I remember a client who I was praying for the day before the session. The Holy Spirit began to give me words of knowledge about her being locked in a prison and specific scriptures to share with her about how He wanted to set her free. The next day, when the session started, I asked her how she felt, and she said, "I feel like I'm in prison."

Practically speaking, when you go to a mechanic or a doctor, they don't just start operating on you. They do an assessment to get a clear idea of what the issue is and what steps they need to take in order to resolve it. That is why it's so important not to miss this step. There may be specific things in the pre-ministry assessment that you may need to address further. Or, the pre-ministry assessment will determine whether a person is even ready to receive inner healing and deliverance. There was a particular client I met for at least seven sessions. Finally, the Holy Spirit revealed to me that she was not willing to forsake her lifestyle and commit to Christ. Even though I felt the Holy Spirit was telling me this, I proceeded to do deliverance. As I began to address the demons, the person sat there and looked at me like I was telling her a bad joke. Even though Jesus

Timothy G. Lane

Christ paid the price for our inner healing and deliverance, God has a pre-requisite. If you don't meet God's conditions for inner healing and deliverance, then you won't receive it. This is exactly what the Apostle James was telling the church that needed healing:

> For as the body without the spirit is dead, so faith without works is dead also.
> ~ James 2:26

During the pre-ministry assessment, you also want to review with the counselee God's condition for healing and deliverance.

God's pre-requisites for inner healing and deliverance are as following:

a)   Willing to forgive from the HEART

> Then his lord, after that he had called him, said unto him, O thou wicked servant, I forgave thee all that debt, because thou desiredst me: Shouldest not thou also have had compassion on thy fellowservant, even as I had pity on thee? And his lord was wroth, and delivered him to the tormentors, till he should pay all that was due unto him. So likewise shall my heavenly Father do also unto you, if ye from your hearts forgive not every one his brother their trespasses.
> ~ Matthew 18:32-35

b)   Willing to repent and forsake all sin

> He that covereth his sins shall not prosper: but whoso confesseth and forsaketh them shall have mercy.
> ~ Proverbs 28:13

52

c)   **Willing to accept Jesus Christ as Lord and Savior**

Neither is there salvation in any other: for there is none other name under heaven given among men, whereby we must be saved.
~ Acts 4:12

d)   **Willing to change habits and commit to new habits**

That ye put off concerning the former conversation the old man, which is corrupt according to the deceitful lusts; And be renewed in the spirit of your mind; And that ye put on the new man, which after God is created in righteousness and true holiness.
~ Ephesians 4:22-24

e)   **Willing to be open**

Confess your faults one to another, and pray one for another, that ye may be healed. The effectual fervent prayer of a righteous man availeth much.
~ James 5:16

f)   **Willing to commit to being faithful to a local church**

Not forsaking the assembling of ourselves together, as the manner of some is; but exhorting one another: and so much the more, as ye see the day approaching.
~ Hebrews 10:25

Before beginning the 7-step model, it is important that the individual understands these things and is willing to commit to them. If not, the sessions will not be successful, or the person will not be able to maintain their freedom. During the pre-ministry assessment, be sure to ask the person if they are willing to accept God's conditions for healing and deliverance in their lives. If at any point the person is not willing to consent to the conditions for healing and deliverance, do not proceed with the inner healing and deliverance. Scripture reminds us to "Give not that which is holy unto the dogs, neither cast ye your pearls before swine, lest they trample them under their feet, and turn again and rend you" (Matthew 7:6). I would also like to point out the following scripture:

> *When the unclean spirit is gone out of a man, he walketh through dry places, seeking rest; and finding none, he saith, I will return unto my house whence I came out. And when he cometh, he findeth it swept and garnished. Then goeth he, and taketh to him seven other spirits more wicked than himself, and they enter in, and dwell there: and the last state of that man is worse than the first.*
> *~ Luke 11:24-26*

This scripture is telling us that if you go through deliverance, but you're not willing to do what it takes to stay delivered, you can end up worse than before. When Jesus healed the man that was paralyzed, he illustrated this by telling him the following:

> *Afterward Jesus findeth him in the temple, and said unto him, Behold, thou art made whole: sin no more, lest a worse thing come unto thee.*
> *~ John 5:14*

Unfortunately, I had to learn this the hard way. I ministered inner healing and deliverance to a former gang banger who was powerfully delivered from at least twenty spirits. A couple of days later, he went home and tried what I did on his mother. When the demons manifested and started growling, he had no idea what to do, so he called me. This was around 11:00 p.m. I rushed to his house knowing that his mother was in an ungodly relationship with a man that she'd been living with for years. Even though she stated she was going to leave him, I had a feeling she wasn't going to follow through, but I proceeded to evict the spirits out of her. The demons were stronger and more resistant, but hours later, they came out. After that incident, there was no change in his mother's life, and I received a call that his mother was being hospitalized. Not only were the spirits tormenting her more, but she began losing her sight and experiencing other physical sicknesses. This was a hard and painful lesson for me to learn. There was another client of mine, due to no fault of mine, who went through deliverance, but days later, she expressed that she was experiencing a sexual attack like she'd never experienced before. Her last state was worse than the beginning. During our next session, I questioned her and found out that even though she stopped having sexual relationships with some of the men, she didn't stop with all. So, those demons returned and were seven times worse. Thank God we were able to address the issue by having her do practical things to disconnect herself with those men *(block their number, unfriend them from Facebook, etc.)* and she was delivered.

SPIRITUAL ASSESSMENT

Besides the pre-ministry evaluation I do before the session, there is a spiritual assessment I do at the beginning of the first session (view Appendix B).

The spiritual assessment's purpose is to assess your spiritual health. Ephesians 6:10 tells us to *"be strong in the Lord, and in the power of his might."* Luke 18:1 says that *"men ought always to pray, and not to faint."* The stronger you are spiritually, the easier the sessions. Also, from my experience, the inner healing and deliverance process flows much simpler when you have healthy daily spiritual habits of reading your Bible, worshipping, praying, and being faithful to your local church. You are better able to see, feel, and hear God during the sessions, and I, as the deliverance minister, am better able to flow in the anointing and the gifts of the Spirit.

Also, when you have a strong spiritual life, the demons that are attached to you are frailer than if you are what the Bible in Romans 15:1 calls *"weak."* When your spiritual life is strong and demons are being cast out of you, their resistance is usually minimal. I was ministering to someone who had severe childhood trauma and as a result was heavily demonized. I knew this person loved God and had a strong spiritual life. They loved to study the Bible and worship, and rarely missed services. As I was going through the deliverance prayer, we barely made it to the third sentence when the demons began to manifest. As I commanded them to reveal who they were and come out, they immediately complied. Some even begged me to "leave us alone" and said, "Please, please don't make us go. Why do we have to go?"

The final reason why it's important for you to have strong spiritual habits is that it is vital to you maintaining your deliverance. After the session is complete, you must take ownership of continuing to build yourself up spiritually through the things listed above and also praying daily in your prayer language. The Bible explicitly instructs every believer to do this in 1 Corinthians 14:4 where it says, *"He that speaketh in an unknown tongue edifieth himself; but he that prophesieth edifieth the church."* In Jude 1:20, it states, *"But ye, beloved, building up yourselves on your most holy faith, praying in the Holy Ghost, Keep yourselves in the love of God, looking for the mercy of our Lord Jesus Christ unto eternal life."* According to the scriptures, you have to take ownership in order to build yourself up in God through praying in tongues.

CHAPTER 6

MAINTAINING YOUR FREEDOM

But ye, beloved, building up yourselves on your most holy faith,
praying in the Holy Ghost. ~ Jude 1:20

In order for inner healing and deliverance to be impactful and lasting, there has to be repentance, transformation, and re-alignment with the word of God. God's word is His covenant or contract with us and states, *"If ye be willing and obedient, ye shall eat the good of the land"* (Isaiah 1:19). There's another scripture that states, *"To obey is better than sacrifice"* (1 Samuel 15:22). Jesus Christ died on the cross and paid the price for our healing and deliverance. Therefore, our freedom is not contingent upon our status, title, or works, but we do have to be in alignment with God's word. Even though God is almighty, He can't do what He wants to do because of the spiritual laws He has established in His Kingdom. God is subject and legally bound to one thing, His word. When we are out of alignment with God's word in our thinking, speaking, or actions, it limits the flow of God's power and gives the devil legal ground to oppress, torment, and demonize us. That's why when Jesus was being tempted by the devil to get out of alignment with God's word, He said, *"Man shall not live by bread alone, but by every word that proceedeth out of the mouth of God"* (Matthew 4:4). This scripture is not just talking about sin. For example, if the Bible says, *"in everything give thanks"* (1 Thessalonians 5:18) or Philippians 4:8 which instructs you to think on things that are good, lovely, or of good report, if you don't do these things you give spirits like depression, torment, and negativity legal access. To be free from these things, you have to repent for being out of alignment with God's word, renounce the thoughts or words you've spoken, and recommit to following God's word. Then the person ministering inner healing and deliverance can pray and bring deliverance. When I am doing deliverance and the demonic spirit is giving me a hard time, I know that the issue is not the power of God. There's something in the person's life that's out of alignment with God's word.

> *Submit yourselves therefore to God. Resist the devil,*
> *and he will flee from you.*
> *~ James 4:7*

I've heard the latter part of this scripture quoted many times while excluding the first sentence. The enemy doesn't flee just because you resist. We can command demons to flee until our face turns blue, but if you're not submitted to God's word, then that spirit has the legal right to stay. If by chance it does flee, it will only come back. This happened while I was doing deliverance on this particular individual. The individual and I were tired because there were so many demons that it was two hours later and the demons were still coming out. The way they were coming out wasn't polite either. They were cursing me, screaming, telling me things like "I hate you," "You're stupid," "I'm stronger than you." None of that concerned me because I know the authority of Jesus Christ that dwells within. The one thing that did concern me was, as one spirit was leaving, it said, "I'll be back." If that was the case, that meant we went through hours of deliverance for nothing. The only way that spirit would be able to come back is if that person went back to the same behavior or ways of thinking that caused the spirit to enter in the first place. In other words, they weren't totally submitted to God's word. That's why it's important to deal with the individual before you deal with the demon. You can cast a demon of lust out of someone, but if that person is not totally repented and is still having ungodly sex, then that spirit is coming back. That's why this 7-step model not only brings inner healing, but is also strategically structured to deal with any legal rights the devil may have because of areas in your life that are not in obedience to God's word. Once you get to the deliverance part, usually within five to ten minutes, demons begin manifesting and coming out because they are too weak and have lost so much ground that it's hard for them to resist the power of Jesus Christ. Even if the demons manifest, the manifestation is nothing like what you see in Hollywood's *The Exorcist* movies. The demons are too fragile to put on a show. I've also experienced, even before I get to the deliverance part, demons beginning to come out of people because they've been dismantled and have nothing to hold on to.

> *But ye, beloved, building up yourselves on your most holy faith, praying in the Holy Ghost, Keep yourselves in the love of God.*
> ~ *Jude 1:20-21*

I would like to dig a little deeper in the scripture mentioned above. Notice in Jude 1:20, the Bible states that it is your responsibility to "keep" yourself. This is important because you don't want to become dependent upon the inner healing and deliverance person, thereby using that individual as your crutch. You have to become self-sufficient by knowing who you are in Christ, which is more than a conqueror (Romans 8:37), and relying on the Holy Spirit to take you through any counter-attacks the devil has set up. The same anointing the minister or counselor uses to bring freedom in your life is the same anointing you have to stay free. As I mentioned before, once you master this model, it can be utilized to do self-deliverance. I remember I was going through one of the toughest situations in my life. Every time it would get tough, I would call my father to rescue me. He became my crutch. He would talk with me, coach me, and pray with me until I felt better. That was momentary, and days later, the situation would flare up again, and I'd call him to get my prayer and counseling medication to calm me down and help me regulate my emotions.

This went on for months. One day, I realized that he wouldn't always be there to rescue me. I needed to learn how to stand on my own two feet and do what David did when he was faced with trouble. The Bible states in 1 Samuel 30:6, *"And David was greatly distressed; for the people spake of stoning him, because the soul of all the people was grieved, every man for his sons and his daughters: but David encouraged himself in the LORD his God."* After realizing this, I called my father and told him that there would be a time where he wouldn't be around, and I couldn't keep using him to keep me emotional and spiritually stable. Please, don't misunderstand me; everybody needs a support system, but that support system can't become your foundation or the ground that you stand on. If they're not reachable or if something happens to them, you will fall apart. I knew my father was there when I needed him, but I began to pray more and seek God myself for guidance and strength. This caused me to put my trust in God and not in people. As a result, I began to become stronger and spiritually independent. I developed my own prayer life so I didn't have to depend on someone else's. I started to dig deeper in the Bible and learned how to hear God for myself and wasn't relying on someone else to tell me what "thus saith the Lord." About a year after I had that conversation with my father, he unexpectedly died of a lung condition. He was no longer available for me to call or get counsel from, or to pray me through. But that was okay because I learned how to keep myself in the love of God (Jude 1:21). If I didn't learn how to do that, I would've fallen apart and the devil would've destroyed me when my father died.

Not only is it important to go through inner healing and deliverance, but you also have to walk in the authority that you already have through Christ. Challenging yourself to learn and utilize the tools or, better yet, weapons that God has given you so that you can defeat the enemy and maintain your freedom is imperative. Once you go through inner healing and deliverance, you have to learn how to do spiritual warfare. This became a serious reality to me when a client came to see me who had a strong history of witchcraft in her family. In our first session, she walked into the room, sat down, and the lights began flickering on and off. I had dealt with some strong demons, but this was my first time experiencing a physical phenomenon of that magnitude. As we began doing deliverance, a strong spirit of witchcraft began manifesting, twisting her body and speaking. To say that she was terrified is an understatement. After the session, she began to experience intense demonic attacks to the point she called me and told me she felt like she was in a *Final Destination* movie. I had to share scriptures with her to help her realize that she doesn't have to be fearful or intimidated by the enemy because Jesus has given us power over all the power of the devil (Luke 10:17). The enemy only can do to us what we allow him to do because of a lack of understating, faith, and usage of the authority we have in the name of Jesus Christ through the power of the Holy Spirit. The following scriptures help us to realize that God has already given us weapons to defeat any demon, no matter how powerful.

> *(For the weapons of our warfare are not carnal, but mighty through God to the pulling down of strong holds;) Casting down imaginations, and every high thing that exalteth itself against the knowledge of God, and bringing into captivity every thought to the obedience of Christ; And having in a readiness to revenge all disobedience, when your obedience is fulfilled.*
> *~ 2 Corinthians 10:4-6*

I have realized and experienced that after sessions are over and the person receives a breakthrough, demons become infuriated. The devil is coming back to see if he can get back in. The devil is coming back to see if the person will fall for the same tricks. If the individual hasn't been properly prepared and maintained themselves through spiritual habits of prayer, Bible reading, and faithfulness to the church, they won't be able to resist the devil properly and biblically. He will gain access or scare the person into not coming back to the sessions. Below, I've provided steps and scriptures of what you have to do to maintain your freedom: (*view Appendix D for more steps*).

a. Change your behavior.

Afterward, Jesus findeth him in the temple, and said unto him, Behold, thou art made whole: sin no more, lest a worse thing come unto thee. ~ John 5:14

Don't go back to the things that caused you to be bound in the first place. This not only includes your actions but your speaking and thinking. If you do, repent, renounce it, and turn away from it immediately.

My little children, these things write I unto you, that ye sin not. And if any man sins, we have an advocate with the Father, Jesus Christ the righteous: And he is the propitiation for our sins: and not for ours only, but also for the sins of the whole world.
~ 1 John 2:1-2

This scripture instructs us that if we do fall back into sin, we can receive forgiveness and restoration through Jesus Christ.

b. Stay full of the Spirit (Holy Spirit).

Praying always with all prayer and supplication in the Spirit.
~ Ephesians 6:18

According to this scripture, we have to pray in tongues daily. This keeps us full of the Spirit of God. When something is full, that means nothing else can get in. As long as you stay full of the Holy Spirit, the enemy will not be able to gain access again.

c. Be faithful to the house of God.

And let us not neglect our meeting together, as some people do, but encourage one another, especially now that the day of his return is drawing near. ~ Hebrews 10:25 NLT

When you neglect the house of God, you miss the corporate blessings God has for you and make yourself vulnerable to the enemy. Also, God has given us pastors as spiritual coverings. Unfaithfulness to your local church causes you to come out of your spiritual covering and exposes you to the enemy.

d. Actively and aggressively resist the devil.

Submit yourselves therefore to God. Resist the devil,
and he will flee from you.
~ James 4:7

e. Know your authority.

Behold, I give unto you power to tread on serpents and scorpions, and over all the power of the enemy: and nothing shall by any means hurt you. ~ Luke 10:19

This scripture lets us know that the devil only can do what you allow, you're his boss. Whenever demonic spirits challenge us, we have to use our authority through the name of Jesus to crush the enemy and his tactics. This is done by giving strong direct commands to demonic spirits who influence our thoughts and feelings.

f. Practice self-deliverance.

If you feel like you have opened a door and have become demonized again, repent, pray in the Spirit, and command that specific spirit to go in Jesus's name. If you still need deliverance, seek a deliverance team for help.

CHAPTER 7

7-STEP GOD THERAPY MODEL

If you are in need of inner healing and deliverance, please contact my staff and me at Lanehelps.com, and we will set up an in-person or video session with you. You can also sign up for the God Therapy Training Academy to begin a training conference at your church or a selected venue or receive personal coaching sessions. The God Therapy Training Academy will provide you with in-depth training to equip you with the knowledge and skills to not only receive inner healing and deliverance, but also to minister inner healing and deliverance effectively and develop your own team. I highly recommend that you go through inner healing and deliverance yourself before ministering inner healing and deliverance to others.

The inner healing and deliverance God Therapy model consists of seven steps:

1. Removal of sin
2. Removing unforgiveness
3. Breaking word curses
4. Removal of generational sins & curses
5. Breaking ungodly soul ties
6. Healing of trauma & grief
7. Deliverance from demons

While going through these prayers, you will experience the presence of God, and if demons are there, you may experience demonic manifestation. Most people are not aware that certain manifestations are demons in disguise. While in the session, if you experience things such as headaches, nausea, body pain, something turning in your stomach, mental blockage, fear, anxiousness, doubt, or hear negative voices in your mind, those are demonic spirits. The rule of thumb is if it's good, it's God, but if it's bad, it's the devil. This is not to scare you, but to build awareness. Usually, before your inner healing session, demons might attempt to disrupt things in your life so you will cancel the session. Things from fighting with your spouse, getting sick, or feeling irritated, agitated, or discouraged from coming are demonic spirits attempting to dissuade you from coming to the session because they are afraid of what Jesus Christ will do during the sessions. Just be determined and relentless and understand that Jesus Christ has already given you the victory, you just have to take it by force.

> *And from the days of John the Baptist until now the kingdom of heaven suffereth violence, and the violent take it by force.*
> ~ *Matthew 11:12*

Materials needed if doing God Therapy:
- Bibles
- Pens
- Notepads
- Tissue
- Paper towels
- Garbage can
- Team of no less than two people

Here are some additional tips when doing God Therapy:

- ABC—always be caring
- Don't depend on yourself; rely on the Holy Spirit.
- Make sure you're not carrying sin or issues into the sessions (demons will transfer)
- You and the team member should arrive fifteen minutes early to set up, pray, and meditate
- Ask the person being ministered to, to arrive at least five minutes early
- When doing deliverance, don't yell or scream. Demons submit to the authority and power you have through Jesus Christ, not how loud you are
- Tell the demons exactly what you want them to do and where you want them to go. (Use commands like, "Don't hurt them," "Be still," "Come out and go to the pit or where Jesus sends you.")
- Don't rush; there's always time for another session

This entire inner healing and deliverance process is focused on bringing healing to your heart, breaking curses, and transforming negative thinking patterns about yourself, God, or a situation to positive patterns of thinking and deliverance from demons. Throughout the process, the team that's doing the inner healing, which consists of two people, should take notes on people who have hurt the person being ministered to (which they will need to forgive), traumatic experiences, and demons that may be present in the individual. Each session should be no longer than an hour and a half. You can utilize the checklist in Appendix C to keep track of where you are in the God Therapy model and pick up where you left off.

I have provided scriptures before each model. It is important that you take the time to read through and understand each scripture. If you're doing inner healing and deliverance, share scriptures with the individual being ministered so you can prepare them for what the Holy Spirit is about to do, build their faith, give them revelation about their situation, get them back in alignment with God's word, and bring proper healing. You do not have to share all of the scriptures. Familiarize yourself with these scriptures and let God lead you as to which scriptures to use.

FREEDOM ENCOUNTERS

During the inner healing and deliverance process, you will be asked to picture Jesus. This is called faith imagery. Picturing Jesus is a way to connect directly with Him. It is amazing to me that as I am coaching people to picture Jesus, they begin to have divine encounters with Him. They will feel, hear, and actually see Him. I've even done this with children and had the same results. There was this one child who, when I asked him to close his eyes and picture Jesus, he began to cry because God's presence began touching him. I asked him what he was crying about, and he replied he didn't know, but he felt warmth going through his body. I have witnessed where some will even have deeper encounters and have visions of Jesus. While picturing Jesus, not only will you begin to see Jesus and feel Him, but He will begin to speak to you as well. You will start to have supernatural encounters with our risen Savior. You will start to encounter His presence and hear His voice. Asking you to picture Jesus also reveals if you are connected to Christ. If you cannot picture Jesus, that could be an indication that there is a spiritual blockage somewhere. As you go through the process, those blockages will be addressed and removed. The freedom and encounters with Jesus that I have seen people receive with this process are surreal.

One of my favorites was a businesswoman who flew in from out of town. Normally, I don't do sessions on Sunday because as a pastor, Sunday is already busy. This time, even though I was exhausted from service, I felt impressed to make an exception. During the inner healing process, we found that the woman was carrying guilt and shame from an abortion she had. The Holy Spirit led me to walk her through each month of her pregnancy as if she never had an abortion. I had her visualize carrying the baby in her womb. Each month, she was instructed to feel the baby growing within her, love on the baby, name the baby, and visualize herself giving birth to the baby. Once she gave birth to the baby, I asked her to hold the baby, tell the baby how much she loves her, and then when she's finished spending time with her child, give the baby over to Jesus. This was an amazing thing to watch as the Holy Spirit began to turn her tears of guilt, shame, and regret into tears of love, joy, and peace. I then walked her through forgiving herself and receiving forgiveness from the child and God. Then the Holy Spirit spoke to her and said she would see her baby in heaven and when she does, her child will give her the biggest hug. Months later, I received a letter in the mail from her, and she said that was a defining moment. Her life was never the same after that session, and she would never forget my assistant and I. She also gave the church a nice donation. Words cannot express the joy and fulfillment I receive from partnering with the Holy Spirit and seeing the profound impact that these sessions have on people's lives.

I want to stress that this is only a format. Make sure the Holy Spirit leads you throughout this entire process. Almost in every single session I have, the Holy Spirit will begin to give me revelations and profound things to share with the individuals. Once, I was in a session, and an older missionary at my church was assisting me. As I began to speak, I could feel the Holy Spirit take complete control, and I began to move in the gift of revelation and words of knowledge. I went from the counselor to being the student because the revelation I was receiving was ministering to me also. I wasn't the only one. After the session, the missionary said to me: "Pastor, I need to give you an offering because I felt like you were ministering to me." I find this process so exciting because you never know what God is going to do. I would suggest if you are doing inner healing and deliverance, be sure to read through the steps you are covering so you can be prepared. Once you familiarize yourself with the seven steps, it will be easy for you to navigate through them.

Begin the inner healing and deliverance process with the following:
1. Pre-Counseling Assessment *(should've been completed by the person being ministered to and scrutinized by the person ministering before the session).*
2. Spiritual Assessment *(This is done by interviewing the person receiving ministry and completed before the 7-step God Therapy model).*
3. Checklist *(completed by the person ministering and done after each session).*

These are found in the Appendix of your manual.

Open the session using the opening prayer.

OPENING PRAYER

Father, in Jesus's name, we thank you and welcome you to this session. We yield this entire session over to you. I bind every spirit from hindering this session. Father, I ask that you release the gifts of the Spirit and bring total deliverance and freedom to this person in Jesus's name. Amen.

CHAPTER 8

STEP ONE: REMOVAL OF SIN

SESSION GOAL:

- Remove sin
- Understand the love of Jesus Christ
- Remove any guilt, shame, rejection, or self-condemnation
- Have a love encounter with God
- Remove demons' legal rights

NOTES:

Sin separates you from God and hinders the healing process. Just because you have sin in your life, this doesn't mean that God doesn't love you. God has unconditional love for you, but He is also bound to His word. The consequences of sin have nothing to do with whether God loves us or not, but has everything to do with

Kingdom laws that God cannot break. Yes, Jesus already paid the price on the cross for our healing and deliverance, but to receive it, you have to repent and forsake sin. If you fall back into sin, it is imperative that you repent and turn from it. Jesus Christ has also purchased all the mercy and grace you may need from God, through dying on the cross. God's grace and mercy will never run out on you. You can come back to Him as much as you need to and He will always welcome you with a smile and open arms.

If you are dealing with guilt, shame, rejection, or condemnation, this will result in a lack of faith in God's desire to heal you and will disconnect you from feeling God's presence or hearing His voice. By thinking God is rejecting you because of your sins, you are really rejecting Him. It's like He wants to hug you, love you, and heal you but you keep pushing Him away because you feel like He doesn't. It's also important for you to understand that what's in your head may be different from what's in your heart or emotions. It's possible for you to think one way in your head and feel another way in your heart. Technically speaking, it's almost like you have two brains: the logical brain (the thinking, rational part of the brain) and the emotional brain (the feeling part of the brain). For example, your religious upbringing and biblical knowledge might cause you to know God loves you theologically, but in your heart or emotional side, there's a wound which feels unloved by God. Or, there is guilt and shame that feels like God has forsaken you because of your past mistakes, even though He said He would never leave nor forsake you. This could be connected to childhood trauma and wounds of not feeling love or getting the attention you needed as a child. As a result, you deal with the feelings of rejection and not being loved and project those feelings onto God. It's not good enough to believe that God loves you in your head; your heart has to know God loves you. That is when the healing and transformation take place. This is done through you dispelling any feelings that God doesn't love you, through using scripture and then having an actual encounter with the love of Jesus Christ. Even though I was raised in the church and knew theologically that God loved me, I use to struggle with feelings that God didn't love me. These feelings fueled my depression and blocked me from receiving the total freedom God had for me. The first three to four years of my Christian walk was filled with God proving to me that He really loved me and breaking that wound of not feeling like I was loved. This was done through me having love encounters with God. There were times when I fell into sin and felt so unworthy, useless, and like God turned His back on me. Then I would encounter His presence. That was Him telling me that my feeling was a lie and the truth was that He loves me unconditionally. Once I finally accepted in my heart that God loved me no matter what I did or didn't do, I learned to love myself and got delivered from depression.

SCRIPTURES

If you are ministering inner healing and deliverance, familiarize yourself with these scriptures and be led by the Holy Spirit on which scriptures to use.

Behold, the Lord's hand is not shortened, that it cannot save; neither his ear heavy, that it cannot hear: But your iniquities have separated between you and your God, and your sins have hid his face from you, that he will not hear. ~ Isaiah 59:1-2

The wicked shall be turned into hell, and all the nations that forget God. ~ Psalms 9:17

He that covereth his sins shall not prosper: but whoso confesseth and forsaketh them shall have mercy. ~ Proverbs 28:13

And they said, Believe on the Lord Jesus Christ, and thou shalt be saved, and thy house. ~ Act 16:31

*For I will be merciful to their unrighteousness, and their sins and
their iniquities will I remember no more. ~ Hebrews 8:12*

*If we confess our sins, he is faithful and just to forgive us our sins,
and to cleanse us from all unrighteousness. ~ 1 John 1:9*

*I in them, and thou in me, that they may be made perfect in one; and
that the world may know that thou hast sent me, and hast loved them,
as thou hast loved me. ~ John 17:23*

*My little children, these things write I unto you, that ye sin not. And if
any man sin, we have an advocate with the Father, Jesus Christ the
righteous: And he is the propitiation for our sins: and not for ours
only, but also for the sins of the whole world. ~ 1 John 2:1-2*

QUESTIONS TO ASK

- Is there any sin in your life?
- What are your sin struggles?
- How does God feel about you?
- What do you feel guilt or shame about?

PRAYER

Step 1 Prayer:

Close your eyes and picture Jesus. What do you see, hear, or feel?

Note: If you can't see, there could be a blockage somewhere. You
may have negative feelings in your heart toward God or think God
has negative feelings toward you. Continue with the prayer and

expect God to give you breakthrough.

Repeat this prayer while picturing Jesus:

Father God, I come to you in Jesus's name. I accept the unconditional love you have for me. You love me so much that you gave your only Son to die so that I can be saved. If I were the only person in the world, Jesus Christ would have still died on the cross. That's how much you love me. I accept and confess Jesus as my Lord and Savior. I repent and turn away from all my sins. I ask that you forgive me for . . . (Name specific sins. If you are ministering to someone and the person doesn't feel comfortable have them name them in their head.)

Father God, by faith in your word, I thank you for cleansing me from all unrighteousness. In the name of Jesus, I renounce and release myself from all guilt, shame, self-blame, self-criticism, etc. I renounce all lies that I am not loved, not forgiven, that God is not with me, and any other lies. I will no longer give into these things. I declare in Jesus's name I am forgiven, saved, and righteous because of the price Jesus paid on the cross with His blood. I am a new creation in Christ, old things are passed away, and I am new. Thank you, Father. Amen.

Step 2 Encounter:

- Now close your eyes and picture Jesus cleansing you from all unrighteousness. What do you feel, see, sense, or hear?
- Ask Jesus, "What do you have for me instead of sin and death?"
- Ask Jesus if there is anything He wants to say to you.

Step 3 Minister's Prayer:

Decree they are forgiven and bless them. (For example, say, "In Jesus's name, because of the price He paid on the cross, I decree that your sins have been remitted as far as the east is from the west. I bless you in Jesus's name to receive all that God has for you because of the price Jesus paid on the cross.")

Let the Holy Spirit lead your prayer.

CHAPTER 9

STEP TWO: REMOVING UNFORGIVENESS

SESSION GOAL:

- Forgive from the heart
- Express and release pain
- Find closure
- Receive inner healing
- Remove demons' legal rights
- Cast out demons connected to unforgivness

NOTES

Most Christians have forgiven from their head, but the Bible says that we must forgive from our hearts. When you forgive from your head and not your heart, the wounds that resulted in what the person has done remain because it abides in your heart. To remove the pain, you have to go from your head to your heart. As you go through this process, it is important not to hold in any emotions but to allow yourself to feel and release the pain. Tears are good. The more you cry, the better. Crying is your body's natural way of relieving and healing you from pain. From interviewing my clients, four methods are used which clients felt brought relief from the pain and brought inner healing:

a. Breathing slow, deep breaths into the pain as it surfaces brings relief and releases the pain.

b. Acknowledging, repenting, and renouncing any bitterness, hatred, or anger they have toward the person.

c. Picturing the offender, recounting the event, and saying what they would say if the person were standing there releases feelings and brings closure.

d. Picturing Jesus, inviting Him to heal the wound, and having a literal God encounter.

During this process, you will give over your pain to Jesus. This process can cause deep inner wounds to surface. If it's too painful, picturing Jesus and giving the pain to Him usually causes the pain to subside or be healed. During inner healing, I usually ask a person what their pain level from 1-10 is. After picturing Jesus and giving Him the pain, I ask them what their pain level is, and it's usually much lower. If you are not willing to face the pain, do a surface level forgiveness by repeating the words, but do not picture the person. If you are ministering inner healing to someone, do not push the person if you see that they are struggling with the pain; some people are not ready to face the severity of their wound.

Some people's pain has been buried so deep for so long that when it surfaces from their subconscious to their conscious, they are not prepared for it and may not be ready to deal with it. That's okay. Sometimes, inner healing happens in levels or layers. The more you're healed, the stronger you'll become, and then you can receive deeper levels of inner healing if need be. Sometimes you may have to go through steps multiple times to bring deeper levels of healing and breakthrough. I've had clients who I went through the forgiveness step in ten minutes, some we were able to do forgiveness in one session, and some I had to go through multiple sessions on forgiving.

Forgiveness can be the longest step in the inner healing model. This can also be the most challenging step for you because you recall wounds of those who probably were close to you or that you trusted. Even though this step can be taxing, if you go through it, you can receive powerful breakthrough and wonderful encounters with Jesus Christ. You know your wound is being healed when the hurt is not as painful. You know your wound is healed when you revisit the wound (the memory, the event, the individual) and there's no pain.

Why is forgiveness so important?
I constantly tell people that forgiveness is not for the person, it's for you. Not only does unforgiveness keep you connected to what the person did, but it also keeps you connected to wounds that resulted from the offense or trauma. You may have moved on physically, but emotionally, you can be stuck in that moment. It is important to forgive because you've been through enough already and owe it to yourself to be free from this person and the agony attached to what this person has done to you. Forgiveness allows Christ to come in and release you from the pain and torment of what they did so you can heal. As stated before, when Jesus Christ heals

you, the memory is there, but there's no pain. Now, your test has become a testimony. When you carry unforgiveness, it gives demons access and a legal right to torment you. So many people suffer from physical sickness, emotional torment, and mental torment because of unforgiveness. Some of the greatest physical healing I've experienced was with people who forgave. I remember I was praying for this woman who was experiencing severe chronic pain. It didn't matter how hard I prayed and how much I prayed, the pain would not leave. Not only would the pain not leave, but the power of God was nowhere in sight. Then I asked her, "Who hurt you?" She began to share with me her traumatic story of being wounded by a person close to her when she was a child. I walked her through a prayer of forgiveness, and within seconds of me praying again, the presence of God came on her and she began to gag and vomit something up. After that, all the pain was gone, and she was totally healed. That chronic pain was actually a spirit of infirmity that was connected to unforgiveness. It didn't matter how much I prayed and called on Jesus, that demon had a legal right to be there because of her holding on to the offense and being in disobedience to God's word, which says forgive. Once she forgave, the devil lost his grip, the blockage was removed, and the healing power of God was able to flow into her.

This is the only step in this model where there are three levels. Each level brings a higher degree of healing but can cause you to encounter the most pain. While ministering to someone, use your discretion and be Holy Spirit led on which level of forgiveness to walk a person through. Remember, forgiveness should take place in your heart. If you go through level one forgiveness and realize it's not touching your heart and the inner wound, that means you have to go to a deeper level. When ministering inner healing, if the person is not willing and ready for a deeper level, doing so can cause more emotional damage, and the person may no longer participate in the sessions. That's why you have to monitor the person's pain level and help them to manage their pain by breathing, talking about what they're feeling, or picturing Jesus and giving Him the pain. I recognized that a lot of people are carrying guilt, shame, embarrassment, and condemnation because they have unforgiveness toward themselves. It is of vital importance that you walk through forgiving yourself. A poor relationship with yourself which includes negative self-talk, low self-esteem, and a lack of self-efficacy can cause you not to forgive yourself for something. I've even dealt with clients who were violated as children and in their childlike mind blamed themselves for what happened. They subconsciously carry that blame into their adulthood. Forgiving yourself is a way to release any negative feelings you have toward yourself even if it's in your subconscious.

There are also Christians who may not express it openly, but they blame God for allowing certain things to happen in their life. Forgiving God for anything you feel He's done against you can release any offense you may have against God and cause you to receive the love and breakthrough God has for you. It is easy for us to blame God for things that happen to us or those we love. I remember I woke up one morning and received a text that someone dear to me that I love was charged with attempted murder. In my mind, I began to accuse God and ask myself why God would allow this to happen. Before this thought got rooted in my heart, the Holy Spirit reminded me that this wasn't God's fault, but where we are in our life is a culmination of the decisions we make. I then realized that God loved this person and was just as hurt as I was. I immediately repented and changed my thinking. Everyone is not able to come to this conclusion and understand the scripture that says the following:

The heaven, even the heavens, are the LORD's: but the earth hath he given to the children of men. ~ Psalms 115:16

People ruin their lives by their own foolishness and then are agnry at the Lord. ~ Proverbs 19:3 NLT

These scriptures inform us that God is in charge of heaven, but He's given mankind authority over the earth. As a result, God is limited to what He can do because He needs our permission and submission. When we sin and don't submit to God's will, not only do we block God out, but we also open the door for demons to come in and steal, kill, and destroy. Not only do our decisions and sins have an adverse impact on our lives, but they also impact those close to us. When Achan sinned, not only was he killed, but his entire family was burned with fire as well (Joshua 7:1-26). This wasn't God's will or fault, but a result of a bad decision Achan made. The good thing is that God is a merciful and loving God and it's never too late to repent, change our ways, and allow God to fix our mess and heal our wounds. When I am ministering to someone in this area, instead of taking the long route to biblically explain why God is not responsible for what people have done to them, having them forgive God is a shortcut to allow them to release any offense they may be holding against God so they can receive healing and deliverance.

After receiving inner healing, the wound can be revisited by picturing the person and imagining what they did to hurt you or talking to someone about what happened to you and seeing if any pain or anger surfaces. You shouldn't be feeling any pain, or the pain should be minimal. If you still feel the pain, you need deeper level healing, or there could be a spirit of hurt, depression, etc., that needs to be cast out. Once this is done, the wound will be healed. When I experienced the murder of my brother, it was a pain that I've never experienced before. The fact that the person was never caught and that my brother hadn't accepted Jesus Christ as his savior caused my hurt to be even worse. At first, I had thoughts of revenge and killing the person that murdered my brother. Instead of dwelling on these thoughts, I made a decision to obey God's word and forgive. As a result, the grieving process didn't last too long, and Jesus Christ healed my heart. I know I am healed because I can talk about the death of my brother with no pain and can honestly say that I love the person who murdered my brother and hope he finds Jesus. I understand that it's not human love that causes me to be able to do this, but the supernatural love of Jesus Christ that dwells in me through the Holy Spirit. I am not bound by hurt, pain, hate, revenge, murder, and grief because true forgiveness brings freedom. This is an extreme example, but imagine if I chose not to forgive in my heart. I would still be carrying that wound. The hurt, grief, and anger would've festered, and then demons of hurt, grief, and anger would've entered. Demonic spirits are attracted to inner wounds, sin, and unhealthy thoughts, and if we carry these things, then it opens the door for demons to come in.

SCRIPTURES

And when ye stand praying, forgive, if ye have ought against any: that your Father also which is in heaven may forgive you your trespasses. But if ye do not forgive, neither will your Father which is in heaven forgive your trespasses. ~ Mark 11:25-26

And his lord was wroth, and delivered him to the tormentors, till he should pay all that was due unto him. So likewise shall my heavenly Father do also unto you, if ye from your hearts forgive not every one his brother their trespasses. ~ Matthew 18:34-35

Then Jesus said, "Come to me, all of you who are weary and carry heavy burdens, and I will give you rest. Take my yoke upon you. Let me teach you, because I am humble and gentle at heart, and you will find rest for your souls. For my yoke is easy to bear, and the burden I give you is light. ~ Matthew 11:28-30 NLT

QUESTIONS: Don't forget to write the answers down.

- Who's hurt you?
- Who's hurt you the most?
- How old were you when they hurt you? Write down the ages.
- How have you hurt yourself?
- How has God hurt you?

Or

Close your eyes. Picture Jesus and say: Jesus who do I need to forgive?

PRAYER

Step 1 Forgiveness

Level 1: In Jesus's name, I forgive you (say their names) for what you did to hurt me.

Level 2: Close your eyes and picture the person who hurt you standing in front of you. Now I want you to say slowly, "[Insert the person's name] you hurt me, and I forgive you."

Level 3: Close your eyes and picture the person who's hurt you. Think about what they've done. Now I want you to say, "[Insert the person's name] in the name of Jesus, I forgive you for [name what they did]."

Close your eyes and picture yourself, Now I want you to say, "I forgive you for [complete the sentence]."

Picture God and say: "In Jesus's name, I forgive God for [mention the things you forgive God for]."

Step 2 (option):

This following step is good if you need closure. It helps to release the pain.

Now, I want you to picture the individual who hurt you. What do you want to say to them?

AFTER FORGIVING REPEAT THIS PRAYER

Father God, I give every hurt and pain connected to what has been done to me to you. Please heal my heart from these wounds. I renounce and reject bitterness, offense, anger, hate, and hurt toward whosoever hurt me, and in the name of Jesus Christ, I free myself from all hurt and damage connected to what was done to me. I command healing to my mind, body, will, and emotions. I command any demonic spirits to no longer torment me and release myself from any demonic bondage and curses connected to what this individual(s) has/have done to me, in Jesus's name.

Step 3 Encounter:

Now close your eyes and picture Jesus and invite Him to come in and take away all the pain. What do you see, hear, sense, or feel?

Ask Jesus if He has something for you. What do you see, hear, sense, or feel?

Step 4 Inquiry:

What is your emotional pain level on a scale of 1-10, ten being the worst?

It should be at a 0-4.

Step 5 Counselor Prayer:

In Jesus's name, I command healing to every wound and release blessing over your life. Every demon connected to the people who have hurt you come out in Jesus name.

(Allow the Holy Spirit to lead your prayer.)

Step 6 Refilling: Recommended if the Process Was Strenuous

Close your eyes, picture Jesus, and pray, "Father God, I ask you to come and give me a fresh refilling of your Spirit." Begin to pray in tongues. If you're having trouble, speak in tongues by faith, and then the Holy Spirit will take over. Here are some supporting scriptures about the importance of Christians praying in tongues.

And they were all filled with the Holy Ghost, and began to speak with other tongues, as the Spirit gave them utterance. ~ Acts 2:4

A person who speaks in tongues is strengthened personally.
~ 1 Corinthians 14:4 NLT

CHAPTER 10

STEP THREE: BREAKING WORD CURSES

SESSION GOALS:

- Break word curses
- Perform positive thought replacement
- Release blessings
- Cast out demons connected to word curses

NOTES

Your thoughts influence your emotions, which drive your behavior. This is called the behavioral triangle. When your emotions become damaged, your thinking can become marred also. Most people who are experiencing negative emotions and behaviors such as depression, anxiety, phobias, or anger have core beliefs that are controlling such emotions and behaviors. In this step, it's important to identify your cognitive distortions and negative belief systems. In order to be healed, break curses, and cancel demons' legal rights, these distortions have to be challenged, changed, and replaced with healthy thinking or what God's word says.

One of the biggest lies I've ever heard growing up is, "Sticks and stones may break your bones, but words never hurt." Our words and the words that people speak over us are more harmful than physical wounds. Physical wounds will sometimes heal within three weeks, but you can carry word wounds for a lifetime. The worse wound is not physical abuse, but verbal abuse, especially if it's from a person that has authority over you, like a parent. I hate when I hear parents cursing at their kids or calling them names like "stupid" or "idiot," because they are causing emotional and mental damage to that child. I remember doing therapy in a school, and I overheard a teacher yelling at a student. In front of the entire class, she told this seventh-grade child that she didn't like him, the teachers didn't like him, and she hates coming to work because of him. It was like she was stabbing him in the heart with an invisible knife. During my counseling groups with children, they've told me that their teachers told them that they never will amount to anything and will be failures in life. We know that all teachers are not this way, but the point I am making is that words that are spoken over you, especially in childhood, can become a part of your identity, your core belief system, and you'll grow up believing and feeling that way. This causes inner wounds and opens the door for a person to become demonized. It's important that when people speak negative words over you, you don't accept them, but speak blessings over yourself.

When I was having my first child my, different people told us how horribly painful childbirth was. We were told that giving birth for the first time is the worst of all and it would be impossible to have a natural birth. They also said that it would take long hours for her to deliver and the doctors probably would have to give her a cesarean section. These people had no ill intention, but the truth of the matter is that they were releasing word curses. I refused to accept what people said and spoke the opposite. When it was time to deliver, we arrived at the hospital, and the first thing the doctor asked was, "Do we want an epidural?" We calmly and bravely said no. Even though the contractions were painful, they were tolerable. She didn't experience intense pain until she had to push, and that lasted for only ten to fifteen minutes. While in the delivery room, the doctor instructed the nurses that it wasn't time for her to deliver the baby and they'd be back to check on us in about two hours. Within ten minutes of them leaving, she said she felt like she needed to push. I immediately contacted the doctor. The doctor and the nurses came in, checked her, and sure enough, it was time! They strapped on their gear, but the doctor noticed a problem. The baby was turned the wrong way. The doctor said she would have to use an instrument to turn the baby the correct way. The doctor then left to get the tools she needed and when she came back, the baby had turned the right way on her own. Within three hours of us being in the hospital, we had a beautiful healthy baby daughter.

In addition to the words other people speak over you, there is power in your words. You can speak curses over yourself. It is of vital importance that you don't accept everything people speak over you, and most importantly, monitor the words that come out of your mouth. A lot of word wounds we carry are self-inflicted wounds. Your words are like doors, and whatever you speak, you give permission to enter and impact your life. One of the reasons I was so depressed as a Christian was because of the hurtful words I constantly spoke over myself. I would tell myself things like "You're stupid," "You idiot," "You're not smart," "You're incompetent." Not only did this cause me to have severe low self-esteem and depression, but I also became demonized with a spirit of depression. Once I renounced these things and changed my thinking and confession, I was totally delivered.

Word curses are things you have spoken out of your mouth or people have spoken against you. What you speak gives the devil or God legal access.

Examples of word curses are as follows: "I will never have kids," "I'm stupid," "I can never do anything right."

Negative beliefs are unbiblical ideologies or beliefs systems. They can be against yourself, others, God, or life.

Examples of negative beliefs: *"I will probably fail," "Nobody likes me," "My marriage probably won't work," "God is upset at me," "All men are . . . ," "All women are . . . ," "My life is cursed."*

As stated above, for you to get delivered and stay delivered, your speaking and thinking have to change. You need to identify word curses/negative beliefs, repent, renounce them, and replace them with the truth.

SCRIPTURES

Now tell them this: "As surely as I live, declares the LORD, I will do to you the very things I heard you say" ~ Numbers 14:28 NLT

Words kill, words give life; they're either poison or fruit—you choose. ~ Proverbs 18:21 MSG

Then touched he their eyes, saying, According to your faith be it unto you. ~ Matthew 9:29

QUESTIONS

What are some negative words that have been spoken over you or you've spoken over yourself?

Or

Close your eyes and picture Jesus, and say: "Lord, what are some negative words or thoughts I have about myself?"

"Lord, what are some negative words people have spoken over me?"

"Father God, what are my negative beliefs about you?"

"Father God, what has the devil spoken over me?"

"Father God, what's the truth?"

PRAYER

Step 1 Counselee Prayer

In Jesus's name, I repent of the negative thoughts and beliefs of *(name them)*.

In the name of Jesus, I repent of the negative things I've spoken *(name them)*.

In the name of Jesus, I forgive _____ for speaking *(name the words over my life)*.

In Jesus's name, I repent for believing and speaking that God *(name negative beliefs and words about God)*.

In Jesus's name, I renounce these words, thoughts, or vows and no longer partner with them.

In the name of Jesus, I command myself to be healed from every wound that has been created because of the words I and others have spoken over me.

I break the power of these curses over my life and release blessings. Father, I commit to speaking and thinking only what your words say, and I refuse to accept what the devil or people say about me.

Step 2 Encounter

- Picture Jesus; ask Him, "Lord, what's the truth?"
- What do you sense, hear, see, or feel?
- Say, "Lord, is there anything you want to say to me?"

Step 3 Counselor Prayer

In the name of Jesus, I break every curse spoken over you by you or any other person in your life.

I bind every spirit that has gained access to your life as a result of these curses, and I release the blessing of God over you because of what Jesus did on the cross. Every demonic spirit connected to these word curses I command you to come out in Jesus name.

CHAPTER 11

STEP FOUR: REMOVAL OF GENERATION SINS & CURSES

SESSION GOALS:

- Understand generation sins and curses
- Break generational curses and sins
- Release generational blessings
- Cast out any generational spirits

NOTES:

While working as a family therapist for residents in the Chicago Housing Authority, I was trained to do genograms for my clients. A genogram is a graphic depiction of a person's family tree. This will allow us to get a picture of hereditary patterns of psychological maladies, social challenges, and addictions. It amazed me how some clients who were dealing with things such as domestic violence, mental disorders, and drug addiction had a family history of the same thing which went back as far as two to three generations. I understand the clinical explanation that this can be due to learned behavior or genetics, but there is also a spiritual dynamic. The actions of your ancestors can open doors for curses, sins, and demon spirits to be passed down through the bloodline. In 2 Samuel 11, David committed adultery and murder. As a result, this released a generational curse of perversion and murder in his family. This led to his firstborn son dying, his daughter being raped by her half-brother, his son Absalom killing his own brother, and then his son Absalom attempting to kill David, until Absalom was killed himself. I was casting a demon out of a person, and the spirit of murder identified itself. This spirit of murder spoke through this person and happily revealed that a severe car accident the client was in a year ago was actually orchestrated by it. I was confused because I knew this Christian personally and knew that they didn't do anything, like kill someone, to allow a spirit of murder to come in. Through my curiosity and the direction of the Holy Spirit, I forced the demon to tell me how it got there. The demon of murder revealed that three generations ago, her grandfather killed someone, which gave it legal right to enter the family line. Once we knew this, I had this person repent for the sins of her ancestors, and within seconds, the demonic spirit came out screaming, and the curse was broken.

This brings me to another point: Even after people give their life to Christ, demons can remain because the Bible instructs us that demons have to be "cast out" (Mark 16:17). If deliverance from demons happened when you received Christ, there would be no need for us to cast out devils. All we would need to do is have people accept Christ, and the demonic spirits would automatically leave. Unfortunately, that is not the case. Once we give our lives to Christ, just like physical sickness and emotional wounds from our past have to be healed, demons also need to be addressed and removed.

Generational sins give you a predisposition for certain sins. What this means is you can be born with an innate desire for a particular sin because of the sins of your parents or ancestors. Some people grow up drawn and enticed to a particular sin because that sin runs in the family. Some of the ones I have witnessed with clients are homosexuality, adultery, rape, lust, molestation, witchcraft, addictions, and murder.

Generation curses are any negative pattern you see in your life and family line. This could be emotional or mental problems (depression, anger, and mental disorders), relational problems, or failures, sickness, etc. Some that I have witnessed while doing inner healing and deliverance are divorce, mental illness, depression, sickness, and poverty. You can inherit physical, mental, and emotional sickness because it has been passed down due to sins and demonic doors that have been opened by your parents and ancestors. It's important while christening a child that the minister prays prayers that break generational curses. Most don't because they have no clue about generational sins, curses, and spirits. If you have children, you don't have to worry; as a parent, you have the authority to break these curses over your child and cast out any demonic spirits that snuck in through the bloodline.

Generation spirits are demons that have been transferred to you because of the sins of your parents or ancestors. These are inherited demons. You don't have to commit the act to have the spirit, because it's inherited. Some of the generation spirits I have encountered while doing deliverance are witchcraft, Jezebel, the spirit of Leviathan, lust, murder, and abortion.

The generational sins have to be repented of; the curses have to be renounced and broken in Jesus's name; the generational demons have to be cast out. It is important not to go through deliverance unless you repent, renounce, and break the generational curses and sins. Generational spirits are usually the strongest, and saying prayers to break these curses weakens them.

SCRIPTURES

And as Jesus passed by, he saw a man which was blind from his birth. And his disciples asked him, saying, Master, who did sin, this man, or his parents, that he was born blind? ~ John 9:1-2

Our fathers have sinned, and are not; and we have borne their iniquities. ~ Lamentations 5:7

Wherefore, as by one man sin entered into the world, and death by sin; and so death passed upon all men, for that all have sinned. ~ Romans 5:12

Christ hath redeemed us from the curse of the law, being made a curse for us: for it is written, Cursed is every one that hangeth on a tree. ~ Galatians 3:13

QUESTIONS:

What are some generational curses and sins that are in your family? (*Write them down*).

What are generational spirits that are in your family line? *(write them down) portion).*

Or

Close your eyes and picture Jesus. Ask Him: "Lord, what are some generational sins, curses, and spirits that have been released in my family?" *(Write them down.)*

PRAYER

Step 1 Prayer:

I confess that Jesus Christ is my savior and I am redeemed by the death, burial, and resurrection of Jesus Christ. In the name of Jesus, I repent of my sins and the sins of my ancestors. I renounce and reject the curses and sins of my parents and ancestors on my mother's and father's side, going all the way back to Adam and Eve. I break every impact these curses and sins have had on my family and me. In Jesus's name, I destroy these curses and sins and loose myself from them because of the shed blood of Jesus on the cross. In Jesus's name, I forbid any curse, sin, and demon from operating in my life and transferring to the next generation. I release generational blessings over myself and my family. I bind every demonic spirit that has been released in my life because of generational curses and sins, and because of the power of the cross and in the name of Jesus Christ, I terminate these curses and sins.

Step 2 Counselor prayer:

In Jesus's name, I break every generational sin and curse. You generational curse and sins of (name the actual curses and sins you or the person wrote down), I command you to go now! I bind every generational spirit and forbid you from operating in this person's life. You generational spirits of (name the actual spirits you or the person wrote down), you will do no more harm to this person and can no longer function in this person's life. I command you to come out in Jesus name and never return. I release generation blessings over (say the person's name) and their family.

Step 3: Inquiry

Did you sense, hear, or feel anything, whether good or bad, while you were praying or while I was praying for you?

CHAPTER 12

STEP FIVE: BREAKING UNGODLY SOUL TIES

SESSION GOAL:

- Understand soul ties
- Break ungodly soul ties
- Remove things you have in your possession that connect you to that person
- Cast out demonic spirits connected to soul ties

NOTES:

A soul tie is a joining or a tie or knitting between two people. *(Close friends, intimate relationships, sexual partners, etc.)* Not only is it a joining, but it is an emotional, mental, physical, and spiritual connection and exchange. Ungodly soul ties can cause a transference of demons; mental, spiritual, emotional, and physical issues; and curses. You can be soul tied not only to a person, but to places and things. Things that may be hard for you to let go of that you know you need to let go of, most likely, are soul ties. I remember praying for a member who was constantly sick. She would get healed but sick again the next Sunday. This went on for months. One day, I felt that it was a spirit of infirmity transferred to her through a soul tie. Once I asked her about this, she affirmed that she was in an intimate relationship with an older man that was an unbeliever. She further explained that he was a very sick person. She told me that it has been difficult for her to detach from him emotionally, and every time he came into town, she fell into sin. After realizing this, I went through the steps to break the soul tie, and a demonic spirit manifested and came out of her. After that, she was totally healed. I instructed her to delete his number and cut off all communications with him, and also discard anything that reminded her of him. If she didn't, the sickness and the spirit would come back.

SCRIPTURES

What? know ye not that he which is joined to an harlot is one body? for two, saith he, shall be one flesh. ~ 1 Corinthians 6:16

And it came to pass, when he had made an end of speaking unto Saul, that the soul of Jonathan was knit with the soul of David, and Jonathan loved him as his own soul. ~ 1 Samuel 18:1

QUESTIONS

What are some unhealthy or ungodly soul ties that you have with people, places, or things? (*Write them down.*)

Or

Close your eyes, picture Jesus, and ask Jesus about some unhealthy or ungodly soul ties you might have with people, places, and things.

PRAYER

Step 1 Prayer & Encounter:

Close your eyes and get a picture of Jesus, and as you pray, picture Him breaking these soul ties.

In Jesus's name, I confess and repent of an ungodly soul tie with (name any person, place, or thing) as a result of _____.

I forgive _____ for their involvement in this sin. I ask you, God, to forgive me, and I forgive myself for participating in this sin.

In the name of Jesus, I sever the ungodly soul tie between me and

_____.

In Jesus's name, I remove anything that has come into me through these soul ties and bring back anything godly that has been stolen from me. I take back anything that I've given and send back anything I've received from these people.

In Jesus's name, I disconnect myself from every ungodly soul tie, and I commit no longer to being in a relationship with this person.

Step 2 Counselor Prayer:

In the name of Jesus, I break every ungodly soul tie and everything that has been transferred to you because of the soul tie; I destroy it. Everything good that was taken from you because of the soul tie, I command it to come back. Every demonic spirit connected to these soul ties I command you to come out now in Jesus name.

Step 3 Inquiry:

What did you sense, hear, or see while we were praying?

CHAPTER 13

STEP SIX: HEALING TRAUMA & GRIEF

SESSION GOALS:

- Achieve inner healing from trauma and grief
- Bring closure to unresolved issues
- Cast out demonic spirits connected to trauma and grief

NOTES

Trauma leaves negative pictures that produce wounds and

demonization. Negative pictures generate negative emotions. Positive pictures create positive emotions. Also, traumatic events cause traumatic mental and emotional damage like with people living with PTSD. When you experience a traumatic event, you have a right to be angry, fearful, and bitter, but you have to choose to address it through the power of the word and prayer, and release any negative feelings you may have toward the person, yourself, or God. Holding on to these things are detrimental to you mentally and emotionally and will keep you in spiritual, mental, and emotional bondage. To be healed, you need to replace the negative picture with a positive one of Jesus's love, mercy, or healing. You need to re-enter the trauma and find out where Jesus was and what He was doing.

It's not about erasing the memory, but healing your memory so there is no pain or grief connected to the memory. Also, it is therapeutic for you to talk about your trauma or grief. Talking is a natural way for you to release, resolve, and heal the pain from your past. God has created our body with a natural capacity to heal itself. The more we expose ourselves to the trauma or grief, the more we become desensitized, and healing can take place. In the God Therapy Training Academy class, I give a detailed explanation and demonstration of this. It also can be very therapeutic for you to give the narrative of your trauma. Only do it if you feel like you are emotionally ready. In order to do this, write down or talk about what happened before, during, and after the trauma. If there was a person involved in the trauma, you picture the person and find closure through saying what you would say to them if they were standing in front of you. You can also say what you would say to God and yourself. This is not about right or wrong, but about you releasing your suppressed pain, fear, or anger through expressing yourself. Once this is done, you need to forgive the person, God, and yourself. Then you can picture Jesus and allow Him to heal the wound.

GRIEF PROCESS

We have healthy grief and unhealthy grief. Healthy grief allows you to mourn, get closure, and heal from the pain of losing something or someone. With healthy grief, after a year or two, the grieving process should be complete, and you should no longer be in mourning. Unhealthy grief causes you to carry grief and experience recurring pain as if the event or death just happened. What also happens is that you can become demonized with a spirit of grief that keeps the memory and the wound fresh. Holding your emotions inside and not releasing them is one of the leading causes of unhealthy grief. That's one reason we call emotions "e-motions" because it's energy that has to be expressed so it can flow or motion through your body. One of the most emotionally and mentally damaging things you can be told not to do during a loss is cry. By holding your e-motions in, they become stationary, which results in you becoming overloaded and overwhelmed, and you will either implode or explode. In the New Testament Jewish culture, people understood the importance of bereavement, and hired mourners to cry with them during a loss. This was for the sole purpose of assisting the grieving person to grieve. They realized that crying was an important process of releasing and healing from the pain.

There are five stages of grief: denial, anger, bargaining, sadness, and acceptance. What happens with unhealthy grief is you get stuck in one of the stages of grief. As a result, you have no closure and will not be able to recover from the pain. Even Jesus went through the natural stages of grief in the Garden of Gethsemane (Luke 22:39-46). He was in shock, grieved, bargained with God, accepted His fate, and moved on. When people don't have any closure and let go, a spirit of grief will come and attach itself to that wound.

The best way to receive inner healing from grief is to allow yourself time to mourn, express your anger, fear, loneliness, or any other feelings, and go through the final stages of grief. It's also important to get closure. A very powerful process for this is to picture the individual you are grieving, express any unresolved issues, forgive them or yourself, say your final words, and release the person to Jesus. My father was the pillar of my family, raised seven children, was full of wisdom, and also was an anointed pastor. Watching him preach was such an experience. He could teach, preach, and then sing a song that would just usher you into the presence of God. He carried such an aura that he could walk into a room filled with strangers and you would immediately respect him and be drawn to him. At the age of 55 and within a matter of months, his health began to deteriorate unexpectedly. I remember his final days. I was at the bank, and I received a distressing call from my mother to come to the emergency room immediately! I quickly left work, and when I walked into the room, I saw my father in a way I had never seen him before. He was lying on the hospital bed in this fragile state, breathing like a man that just got through a marathon. All I could remember hearing was the different hospital machines beeping like crazy. I looked at my mother, and she had this confused, distressed look on her face. The doctors walked in and asked us what we wanted to do because his heart could give out at any minute. We had to make a decision for the doctors to put him on a ventilator or give him some medication that would let him die without pain. Wow! This was my first time experiencing this, so I had no idea what a ventilator was. They explained that they would have to make him unconscious, and put a tube down his throat so the machine could breathe for him. He was conscious at this time but couldn't talk. The doctors informed us that even if they put him on a breathing machine, he still might not make it. To tell you I was shocked and distraught is an understatement. My mother asked me what to do, and I said I didn't know. We asked my father what to do, and he shrugged his shoulders saying he didn't know. Finally, we decided to put him on the breathing machine. After that, I never saw him conscious again. I would visit his room daily and sit next to his bed and pray and tell God I knew He was not going to take my father.

There were many nights where I just sat next to him and cried in unbelief. It became so emotionally and mentally draining that I told God to either heal him or take him because I could no longer bear the pain of knowing my father was unconscious, with a tube down his throat, on a machine that was breathing for him. Within a day or two, we got the call that he had transitioned. I took my time to explain this to you so that you can get a sense of the trauma and grief I was under. After that incident, I didn't get a chance to grieve because at the tender age of twenty-nine, I became the pastor of the seventy-year-old church. As a result, I carried the trauma and grief for years. I would have dreams that he was alive and in the pulpit preaching, and then wake up and realize he was gone. I would wake up and want to call him and then realize he was gone. I would go to church, walk in the pastor's office, and realize he was gone. This became overbearing, and I began to call out to God for deliverance. Once I was asleep, and two angels appeared to me and walked me through the process that I am about to share with you. I think God did that because there was no one I could go to that understood how to heal me from my grief and trauma. After the dream with the angels, I woke up with tears in my eyes, feeling the healing presence of God. My grief and trauma turned to joy and peace.

SCRIPTURES

Surely he hath borne our griefs, and carried our sorrows: yet we did esteem him stricken, smitten of God, and afflicted. ~ Isaiah 53:4

Blessed are they that mourn: for they shall be comforted. ~
Matthew 5:4

God is our refuge and strength, a very present help in trouble. ~
Psalms 46:1

QUESTIONS

- What traumatic thing has happened to you?
- What are you still grieving about?
- How does it impact you?
- Are there any lies connected to what they did?

Or

Close your eyes and picture Jesus. Now say, *"Father God, what traumatic things have happened to me? What am I still grieving about? What are the lies connected to this hurt?"*

5-STEP PROCESS TO HEALING GREIF AND TRAUMA:

1. Experience the trauma or grief. *(Enter the scene of the wound. Picture what was happening before, during, and after the event.) (When you start feeling pain, take deep breaths and breathe into the pain. This helps relieve and release the pain.)*

2. Picture the individual who is connected to the trauma or grief. Say what you want to say to them. Acknowledge and release any anger, pain, or bitterness. *(If ministering inner healing and the person needs to scream or yell, do not judge; just let them release.)*

3. Forgive whoever needs to be forgiven. *(Individuals, themselves, or God. It may be anger toward God, bitterness toward the offender, or blame toward self.)*

4. Close your eyes again and go back to the scene. Now picture Jesus in the scene. Give Him the pain and receive His comfort and love.

5. Identify unhealthy beliefs about yourself, your life, people, or God that you've developed as a result of the trauma or grief. What impact does thinking that way have on you, your life, and your relationships? Choose to let go, change the way you think and adopt a new healthy belief system.

Finally, brethren, whatsoever things are true, whatsoever things are honest, whatsoever things are just, whatsoever things are pure, whatsoever things are lovely, whatsoever things are of good report; if there be any virtue, and if there be any praise, think on these things. ~ Philippians 4:8

PRAYER MODEL FOR HEALING TRAUMA & GRIEF

It's important that during this process, you do not suppress any feelings. Allow them to surface.

STEP 1: Close your eyes and Re-enter the trauma or event that caused grief or the scene where the wound occurred.

What do you see, feel, or hear?

STEP 2: Picture the individual who the trauma or grief is connected to. Say what you want to say to them.

Anything you want to say to God or yourself?

STEP 3: In Jesus's name, I forgive *(name the person)* and release any *(name the negative feelings)* I have toward them.

In Jesus's name, I forgive myself and release *(name the negative feelings)* I have toward myself.

In Jesus's name, I forgive God and release any *(name the negative feelings)* I have toward God.

In Jesus's name, I confess and repent of any anger, bitterness, or sins I have against myself, the person, and God for allowing this event to happen. I renounce these things in Jesus's name and will no longer partner with negative thoughts about this person, myself, or God regarding this situation.

STEP 4: Go back into the scene. Ask Jesus to show you where He is. What do you think, feel, hear, or see?

Picture Jesus healing the wound, and give Him the pain and receive His comfort and love.

Ask Jesus what He has for you instead. What do you think, feel, hear, or see?

STEP 5: Counselor prayer:

In the name of Jesus, I place the cross of Christ between this person and the grief or trauma and declare freedom from all emotional or spiritual damage stemming from it.

In Jesus's name, I speak healing to every wounded emotion and thought as a result of this traumatic event. I destroy every demonic and ungodly impact this trauma or grief has had on this person. I bind all spirits of grief and trauma and command you to no longer torment this person or operate in their life. In Jesus's name! I release the peace, joy, and love of God upon this person and declare them free in Jesus's name! Every spirit connected to grief our trauma I command you to come out in Jesus name.

STEP 6 Refilling (recommended if the process was strenuous)

Close your eyes, picture Jesus, and pray: "Father God, I ask you to come and give me a fresh refilling of your Spirit." Begin to pray in tongues. If you're having trouble, speak in tongues by faith and then the Holy Spirit will take over.

CHAPTER 14

ADDITIONAL MINISTRY TECHNIQUES

If you find yourself stuck or still struggling, here are some additional techniques that I've found very useful.

The Wounded Warrior Technique

Nay, in all these things we are more than conquerors through him that loved us. ~ Romans 8:37

Behold, I give unto you power to tread on serpents and scorpions, and over all the power of the enemy: and nothing shall by any means hurt you. ~ Luke 10:19

This may feel awkward at first, but it works. Naturally and spiritually, each Christian has a warrior on the inside. Naturally, we have a flight or fight automatic response mechanism. This means that when you are faced with danger, you will either run toward it (like David did Goliath) or run away. Spiritually, Jesus Christ lives within every believer, and He is the Lion of Judah. When it comes to facing painful situations, you can choose to be a wimp or a warrior. You can decide to be a victim or a survivor. A perfect example of this concept is given in 1 Samuel 17. When the Children of Israel were faced with Goliath, who was the Philistine champion and giant, they ran. Then we hear about this young ruddy shepherd boy named David. Instead of running away from the giant, he ran toward and slew him. You see, a lot of people haven't tapped into the warrior inside, especially those who have inner wounds, low self-image, or are demonized. With this technique, you are challenging yourself to go from being a victim to being the warrior you were created to be.

Close your eyes and recall a painful event or trauma and point to the area on your body where you feel the pain. If it was in a form, what would it look like? If it had a voice, what would it say or sound like? This is a method that allows you to connect your mind with your body. We naturally dissociate ourselves from the mind-body connection to bury the pain. In order to relieve the pain, you have to bring it to the surface and release it. Allow yourself to be the victim and be weak.

Now, just like there's someone inside of you that has been victimized, there is also a warrior inside of you, according to the scriptures. Make a decision that you're no longer going to be the victim, but choose to tap into the warrior on the inside. Close your eyes and picture that warrior. What does he or she look like? Picture the Lion of Judah, Jesus living within you. What does He look like? Now, if that warrior had a voice, what would he say? Now, say it repetitively out loud with passion and conviction.

Think about the risk of being a victim. How has that worked for you? What has being a victim accomplished for you? What will happen if you keep living your life like a victim? Think about the benefit of you being the warrior that Jesus has called you to be. What commitment can you make to yourself and God to do Ephesians 6:10, *"Finally my brethren, be strong in the Lord, and in the power of his might,"* and not live your life like a victim.

Truth vs. Lies

And ye shall know the truth, and the truth shall make you free. ~ *John 8:32*

If the "truth makes you free," then lies keep you in bondage. To be totally healed and delivered, you have to make a heart decision to no longer partner with the lies. There is a cognitive distortion called *emotional reasoning*. This is when you think something is true because you feel like it's true. E-motions are fickle and can be damaged. There are usually negative thoughts connected to those negative emotions. It's important to do what I call *emotional connecting* and think about what happened in your past that could have caused the emotional damage or dysfunction in your present. If you follow your feeling or thoughts instead of accepting God's truth, you will not experience freedom and give demons permission to dominate that area of your mind, emotions, and life. What needs to happen is what is called *reframing*. This is where you challenge those distorted ideologies that you feel are true and replace them with God's truth. Then adjust the way you think or speak from a negative tone to a positive one. For the new message to get into your heart and to experience profound freedom, you might have to find scriptures to support your new way of thinking and meditate on those scriptures daily. The following scriptures show us the power and blessings of consistently meditating on God's word and speaking His word over ourselves:

Blessed is the man that walketh not in the counsel of the ungodly, nor standeth in the way of sinners, nor sitteth in the seat of the scornful. But his delight is in the law of the Lord; and in his law doth he meditate day and night. And he shall be like a tree planted by the rivers of water, that bringeth forth his fruit in his season; his leaf also shall not wither; and whatsoever he doeth shall prosper. ~ Psalms 1:1-3

This book of the law shall not depart out of thy mouth; but thou shalt meditate therein day and night, that thou mayest observe to do according to all that is written therein: for then thou shalt make thy way prosperous, and then thou shalt have good success. ~ Joshua 1:8

I remember when I first became a Christian, I struggled with anger. It seemed like I couldn't break loose from it and it would take control of me at times. I found scriptures that talked about anger, and I meditated on them daily. Within months, I was totally free.

In order to be delivered, you have to reject the lies and speak the truth on a consistent basis. Every time those negative thoughts come to your mind, you have to rebuke them, renounce them, and replace them with the truth of God's word.

- Write down the negative feelings you have about yourself or somebody else.
- Where were they birthed? Where do you recall first feeling them?
- What is the negative belief about yourself? (Example: I'm incompetent, I'm stupid, God's not with me)
- Now, what's the truth? Find supporting scriptures.

Or

- What is the message the pain is telling you about yourself? "It's my fault," or, "I'm no good."
- What's the heart's belief about God? "God doesn't love me."
- Now, what's the truth? Find supporting scriptures.

Or

- Picture Jesus and ask Him what the lies are. Then ask Jesus what the truth is.
- Accept the truth into your heart and find supporting scriptures.
- Make a commitment to reject the lie and believe the truth.

PRAYER:

In Jesus's name, I repent for believing the lie of (name the lies or unhealthy beliefs); I renounce it and break the curses connected to it. I acknowledge that by believing these lies, I keep the wound alive and give demonic spirits permission to operate in my mind, will, emotions, and body. I break this agreement with demons and commit to speaking the truth of God's word. Jesus, I ask you to come and heal every pain connected to these lies and replace them with your healing and blessings.

Close your eyes and picture Jesus healing the wound. What do you see, hear, or feel?

Holy Spirit Come Technique

I've found this to be a very simple but powerful technique for bringing restoration, strength, and breakthrough to your life. Dealing with inner wounds and demons can be very draining mentally, emotionally, spiritually, and even physically. From my experience, this technique accomplishes the following things:

a. Allows you to immediately tap into the anointing of the Holy Spirit (Isaiah 10:27 KJV)

b. Removes mental and emotional blockages

c. Weakens demons

d. Revives you mentally, emotionally, spiritually, and even physically

e. Releases breakthrough into your life

As you began to pray in your prayer language, the presence of God will begin to fill you and free you.

SCRIPTURES

And it shall come to pass in that day, that his burden shall be taken away from off thy shoulder, and his yoke from off thy neck, and the yoke shall be destroyed because of the anointing. ~ Isaiah 10:27

But ye, beloved, building up yourselves on your most holy faith, praying in the Holy Ghost. ~ Jude 1:20

I indeed baptize you with water unto repentance. but he that cometh after me is mightier than I, whose shoes I am not worthy to bear: he shall baptize you with the Holy Ghost, and with fire. ~ Matthew 3:11

Verily I say unto you, Whatsoever ye shall bind on earth shall be bound in heaven: and whatsoever ye shall loose on earth shall be loosed in heaven. ~ Matthew 18:18

Close your eyes and picture Jesus. Then pray the following:

"Jesus Christ, I ask you to baptize me with the Holy Ghost and fire, according to your word in Matthew 3:11. I ask you for complete restoration, breakthrough, and deliverance."

Prayer the minister can pray:

In the name of Jesus Christ, according to Matthew 18:18, I release the fire of the Holy Spirit all over you and within you. In Jesus's name, be restored, revived, and set free.

Instruct the individual being ministered to, to pray in tongues, and then you pray in the Spirit with them. If they're having problems, instruct them to speak in tongues and trust that the Holy Spirit will take over.

And they were all filled with the Holy Ghost, and began to speak with other tongues, as the Spirit gave them utterance. ~ Acts 2:4

As the person is speaking in tongues and experiencing God's presence, you can sporadically ask them what they feel, hear, or see. Also, be led by the Holy Spirit, because He might give you words of knowledge, prophecy, etc.

CHAPTER 15

STEP SEVEN: DELIVERANCE

SESSION GOAL:

*   Get a basic understanding of the demonization
*   Understand how to maintain your freedom
*   Cast out demonic spirits

NOTES:

What are demons?

Simply stated, demons are evil spirit beings or evil ghosts. There are debates about where they came from, which I will not get into. The important thing you need to know is that demons are real.

Be sober, be vigilant; because your adversary the devil, as a roaring lion, walketh about, seeking whom he may devour. ~ 1 Peter 5:8

It's a biblical fact that there is an unseen spiritual world within your natural world that's filled with demonic spirits. These demons roam around you like a lion, seeking to gain access to your life. Demons can occupy your mind, emotions, and body. Wherever demons are present, there is discomfort, dysfunction, and destruction.

What causes demonization?

There are certain things you can do or things that can happen to you that open the door for demons to come in. Here are a few: drugs, constant sinning, rape, molestation, verbal abuse, physical abuse, hatred, unforgiveness, bitterness, anger, rebellion, curses, making vows, psychic reading/witchcraft, words that we speak, generational sins and curses, soul ties, trauma, and grief.

What's their assignment?

Demons goals are to do three things—steal, kill, and destroy.

The thief comes only to steal and kill and destroy; I have come that they may have life, and have it to the full. ~ John 10:10 NIV

Whenever and wherever demons are present within your life, they are working to accomplish those three objectives. They do this by attacking and influencing you mentally, emotionally, physically, and spiritually. Many people suffer in these areas because of demons. Here's a few things that can indicate that you or someone you know has a demon: chronic unexplained or seasonal sickness and pain, mental illness; constant depression, fear, anger, hatred, irritation, or anxiety; maladaptive behaviors that you seem to have no control over or that seems overpowering, intrusive, or ruminating evil or negative thoughts; violent behavior, obsessive compulsive behavior, strong pressure to do wrong, constant nightmares, trouble sleeping, feeling of losing control, drug/alcohol abuse, grief, isolation, not able to read your word, pray, praise God, and get a spiritual breakthrough.

There was a lady that came to my church who suffered from a condition where she could not stop shaking. She went to many doctors, they ran tests and could not figure out what was going on. The reason is that it was demonic. When she came to me and explained the situation, I realized that it was a demon. As I began praying for her, she started shaking uncontrollably and was in intense pain. As I kept persistently praying, the shaking stopped, and all the pain left her. She never suffered from that condition again. Demons don't just work internally; they also work externally and destroy people's marriage, ministry, family, career, finances, etc.

Can Christians be demonized?

I do not believe Christians can be possessed, under the complete control of a demon, but I do believe that there is biblical evidence that believers can be demonized. This means that demons are occupying and operating in an area in a believer's life, either internally or externally.

Neither give place to the devil. ~ Ephesians 4:27

Even Paul the Apostle stated that because of an issue around pride, his body was tormented by a spirit of infirmity.

And lest I should be exalted above measure through the abundance of the revelations, there was given to me a thorn in the flesh, the messenger of Satan to buffet me, lest I should be exalted above measure. For this thing I besought the Lord thrice, that it might depart from me. And he said unto me, My grace is sufficient for thee: for my strength is made perfect in weakness. Most gladly therefore will I rather glory in my infirmities, that the power of Christ may rest upon me. ~ 2 Corinthians 12:7-9

Do I have to be afraid of demons?

As a Spirit-filled believer, there is nothing you have to be afraid of. Demons are masters at deception and attempt to make Christians feel fearful and powerless when it comes to overcoming them. The Bible tells us we are *"more than conquerors"* through Jesus Christ (Romans 8:37). Sometimes, demons will put up a fight, but as you persevere in the name of Jesus, they must obey.

Wherefore God also hath highly exalted him, and given him a name which is above every name: That at the name of Jesus every knee should bow, of things in heaven, and things in earth, and things under the earth; And that every tongue should confess that Jesus Christ is Lord, to the glory of God the Father. ~ Philippians 2:9-11

Nay, in all these things we are more than conquerors through him that loved us. ~ Romans 8:37

It is through the finished work of the cross and through the name of Jesus Christ that believers have power over all the power of demons. Evil spirits can only do what you allow them to do. They only gain as much ground as you give them as a believer. Not only do you have the name of Jesus Christ and the power of the Holy Spirit as weapons, but there are also angels that can be released to assist you in fighting against the devil. There were many times while doing deliverance I felt tired, and through the direction of the Holy Spirit, I released angels to attack the spirits. As I sat back and rested, I observed the demons within the person scream and cover themselves in torment as an unseen supernatural force flogged them. The following are scriptures to show you your authority and covering as believers.

And the seventy returned again with joy, saying, Lord, even the devils are subject unto us through Thy name. ~ Luke 10:17

Behold, I give unto you power to tread on serpents and scorpions, and over all the power of the enemy: and nothing shall by any means hurt you. ~ Luke 10:19

All nations compassed me about: but in the name of the LORD will I destroy them. ~ Psalms 118:10

For the angel of the LORD is a guard; he surrounds and defends all who fear him. ~ Psalms 34:7 NLT

As the mountains are round about Jerusalem, so the LORD is round about his people from henceforth even for ever. ~ Psalm 125:2

Instructions for the person doing deliverance:

- Make sure there's no sin in your life
- Make sure you've prayed in the spirit and worshiped
- Be loving
- Periodically stop to investigate, ask them what they feel, hear, or see
- Attempt to get the names of the spirits
- Rely on the total authority of Jesus Christ and the work of the cross

- Don't do deliverance by yourself
- Be aware of demonic attacks/temptations before during or after ministry (temptations, irritations, marital conflict, depression, discouragement, and things happening wrong). All can be and most likely are demonic attacks. Resist these things. Know your authority in Christ

Deliverance tips:

- Make sure it's a quiet, safe place
- Be relentless
- Give exact commands to the demons in Jesus's name
- Release the anointing
- If deliverance is difficult, have the person pray in the Spirit (weakens the demons)
- Stay in control; demons must obey you
- Be gentle and loving to the person
- Stop to interview the person (How are you? You need anything? What do you hear, feel, think?)
- Sometimes one deliverance session is not enough. Follow up with the person to see how they are doing
- Follow the Holy Spirit
- Afterward, release the anointing and fill the person back up with the Holy Spirit. Have them pray in tongues and worship for a few minutes
- Quote scriptures
- Release the fire of God and torment demons (weakens demons).
- Send the demons to the pit
- Pray that warring angels are released to smite the demons
- Keep your eyes open; stay focused on the individual and what's happening

Common ways demons depart:

- Without any manifestations, but the person feels lighter, clearer, and free or feels something leaving them
- Through the mouth (coughing, yawning, sighing, burping, screaming, heavy breathing, vomiting)
- Through the eyelids flickering, eyes rolling in the back of their head, and tears
- Through the head, often accompanied by a sense of tightness and then sudden release
- Through the hands or fingertips, often accompanied by claw-like movement or shaking
- Through the anus by passing gas
- Through the nose/through blowing of the nose
- Through the genitals

Problems that will hinder deliverance:

- Unconfessed issues (never mentioned they were raped or molested and walked through forgiveness)
- Unconfessed sin
- Religious ego
- Belief system (don't believe Christians can be demonized, don't believe they have a demon)
- Weak spiritual life
- Lack of faith
- Still in agreement with the spirits in some way
- Not resisting
- Don't want to be delivered

Additional scriptural instructions for casting out evil spirits:

Bind the strongman.
Or else how can one enter into a strong man's house, and spoil his goods, except he first bind the strong man? and then he will spoil his house. ~ Matthew 12:29

Command spirits to come out and tell them where to go.
For verily I say unto you, that whosoever shall say unto this mountain, Be thou removed, and be thou cast into the sea; and shall not doubt in his heart, but shall believe that those things which he saith shall come to pass; he shall have whatsoever he saith. ~ Mark 11:23

Command demons to submit and obey.
Therefore, God elevated him to the place of highest honor and gave him the name above all other names, that at the name of Jesus every knee should bow, in heaven and on earth and under the earth, and every tongue declare that Jesus Christ is Lord, to the glory of God the Father. ~ Philippians 2:9-11 NLT

Pull down strongholds.
For the weapons of our warfare are not carnal, but mighty through God to the pulling down of strong holds. ~ 2 Corinthians 10:4

Cast out demons.
And these signs shall follow them that believe; In my name shall they cast out devils; they shall speak with new tongues. ~ Mark 16:17

Before doing deliverance, go over the Maintaining Your Freedom handout in Appendix D.

As you prepare to begin administering deliverance, share these

instructions with the person getting deliverance:

- Don't pray audibly.
- Share with me any sensations you feel or see, urges, or voices while being prayed for.
- Allow spirits to manifest, speak, and depart; don't hold things in.
- Don't suppress any impulses you may have. (Just like you can quench the Holy Spirit, you can quench demonic spirits.)
- Be aware of any negative thoughts, feelings, or sensations, and tell me.
- Let me know of any physical pain you are encountering.

DELIVERANCE PRAYER

For a person receiving deliverance, have them repeat this prayer:

In the name of Jesus Christ, I decree and declare that I have power over all the power of the devil. I declare that I am more than a conqueror and no weapon formed against me shall prosper. I declare that if I resist the devil, he will flee from me and in the name of Jesus I resist all demonic spirits and command them to come out of me in Jesus's name. I declare that demons are subject to me through the name of Jesus Christ and must obey my every command. I release the fire of the Holy Spirit all over my mind, body, soul, and spirit, and command every spirit that's attached to me to be tormented. I bind all demonic spirits and command you to name yourself, manifest, and come out of me in Jesus's name. I give you no rest, and I release all the weapons of my warfare through the power that works in me and command every demon to manifest, name yourself, and come out NOW IN JESUS'S NAME. Jesus, I welcome your power, anointing, to be released and destroy all the works of the devil in my mind, body, soul, and spirit.

Have the person name specific spirits and command them to come out.

Stop and interview: Ask the person what they felt, heard, sensed, or saw.

PERSON PERFORMING DELIVERANCE:

In the name of Jesus Christ, I command all spirits not to transfer, linger, but to go to the pit. I forbid you spirits from hiding, but I call you to the surface. I command all demonic spirits to manifest, name yourself, and come out in Jesus's name. I release the tormenting fire of the Holy Spirit all over (say the person's name) against every demonic spirit. I command every spirit to look at the face of Jesus Christ and be tormented and come out. COME OUT IN JESUS'S NAME and go to the pit. In Jesus's name, I command all spirits that came in because of sin to come out. I command generational spirits to come out. I bind the strongman and command all chief spirits to come out. I release the fire of the Holy Spirit and command torment on you demons and command you all out.

REPEAT COMMANDS WHILE NAMING SPECIFIC SPIRITS.

Aftercare Instructions:

Going through deliverance can be very draining mentally, emotionally, and spiritually. Also, demons will attempt to counter attack because of the ground they've lost. After deliverance give the individual the following instructions:

- Strengthen your body: Make sure you eat a good meal and get some rest.
- Strengthen your soul: Psalms 23:2-3 tells us the need for our

souls to be restored. Listen to soft worship music or inspirational things; do something fun and relaxing with someone you love.

- Strengthen your spirit: Read the word of God, build your spirit through praying in tongues, and contact the deliverance minister if you need more prayer and support.

CHAPTER 16

BUILDING YOUR OWN TEAM

To build your team and receive effective training, it is highly recommended that you go through our God Therapy Academy. Visit Lanehelps.com for more info. This training will include all of the materials, documents, and support needed to begin your own inner healing and deliverance ministry.

Jesus sent His disciples out by twos. No one ministered alone. It's important to work as a team for purposes of support, covering, and accountability. The team should consist of males and females. If you are ministering to the opposite sex, a person the same sex as the person you are ministering to should be present. The team leader is the one ministering inner healing and deliverance. The team's assistant's duty is to pray for the team leader that God will cover them, direct them, and release the gifts of the Spirit. Also, pray for the person receiving inner healing. Throughout the process, the support person should be praying and providing assistance for the Team Leader as instructed. The Team Leader might need the assistant to do things such as write something down, get water or paper towels, etc. The support person should not be praying out loud or interrupting the session. If the support person feels like God is showing them something, they should write it down and hand it to the team leader at an opportune time. The team leader has to use their discretion whether they want to share the information or not.

Who should be on the team? What are their characteristics, qualities, and qualifications?

Here are my suggestions:

- Must be Spirit filled, faithful to the local church, and on time.
- Must be submissive to the authority of their pastor.
- Must have a sincere love for people.
- Must complete the inner healing and deliverance training academy.
- Must go through the God Therapy model themselves to receive inner healing and deliverance.
- Must sit in on sessions as an observer in training until the team leader or pastor feels they are ready.
- Must serve as a support person until the team leader or pastor feel they are ready to take a lead role.
- Upon taking a lead role, this person should be observed and later on critiqued by the team leader.

God has called the body of Christ to minister inner healing and deliverance. Preferably, teams should be assembled from members of the local church and with the approval and blessings of the local pastor.

Anyone in the congregation can start the team, but it is recommended that you have the pastor's approval, blessings, and covering.

If you feel you are called to the ministry, you can share with your pastor your vision, your step-by-step plan, and how you feel it would enhance the ministry. If you have a pastor that is resistant because they feel that Christians cannot be demonized, they will probably be against you starting an inner healing and deliverance ministry. If this is the case, you will have to seek God's direction and be led by the Holy Spirit as of what to do. I was a senior pastor and did not believe Christians could be demonized, but some members did. Members and I would have debates about this topic, but I could not be convinced that a "saint" could have a demon. A member prayed to God that He would show me Himself. That's exactly what happened. Through dreams, Holy Spirit led biblical revelation, and actual encounters I experienced with Christians being demonized, I became a believer. It drastically changed the way I did ministry and counseling. It opened my eyes to the members of my church who had struggles and challenges that I could not understand or help, and why. Now, through doing inner healing and deliverance, I have seen members healed from emotional wounds, mental wounds, and demonic bondage. I've also seen them healed from physical sicknesses. As a pastor and therapist, realizing that Christians can be demonized was the missing piece to the puzzle of my ministry/career and allowed me to minister to the people I shepherd on an entirely new level. If your pastor doesn't believe in Christians being demonized, I will challenge you to challenge him or her to read this book.

On a more informal note, the Bible instructs us to cast out devils in His name (Mark 16:17). You don't have to develop a formal inner healing team, but you can partner with an individual in the church and utilize this manual to bring inner healing and deliverance to those in need by just offering them prayers. If you are a ministry leader in any capacity, your pastor might be more understating with that approach rather than you telling him or her that you want to start a ministry. As you began to do inner healing and deliverance, the impact it has on people will cause the ministry to grow, and eyes have not seen where God will take you. As you do it, I believe God will open doors for you, just like He did for me.

Inner healing and deliverance is a Kingdom lifestyle. Teams should commit themselves to being lifelong learners through the consistent study of scriptures, attending training sessions, reading books, and ministering inner healing and deliverance. Here is a list of books or resources that would be helpful for learning more about inner healing and deliverance:

- *Deep Wounds, Deep Healing* by Charles H. Kraft
- *Two Hours to Freedom* by Charles H. Kraft
- *Defeating Dark Angels* by Charles H. Kraft
- *The Biblical Guide to Deliverance* by Randy Clark, DMin.
- *They Shall Expel Demons* by Derek Prince
- *4 Keys to Hearing God's Voice* by Mark Virkler
- *Prayers that Heal the Heart* by Mark Virkler
- Greatbiblestudy.com

-

APPENDIX A

CONFIDENTIAL PRE-MINISTRY ASSESSMENT

Write or circle all numbers of the following symptoms that apply. Please complete and return this assessment at least a day prior to the sessions.

Stomachaches	Seeing or hearing things
Muscle tension	Eating difficulties
Trouble sleeping	Sleeping all the time
Trouble concentrating	Tired
Rapid heartbeat	Dizziness

Aggressive behavior	Suicidal thoughts or attempt(s)
Impulsive behavior	Nervous or anxious

Flashbacks	Nightmares
Unusual repeated behaviors	Use of drugs or alcohol or other Addictions
Sin struggles	Ungodly sexual behaviors

Feeling fearful	Feeling helpless
Feeling angry	Feeling numb/disconnected
Feeling sad/depressed	Feeling confused/unable to focus
Feeling irritable/moody	Being doubtful or negative
Feeling exposed/vulnerable	Feeling ashamed/embarrassed
Feeling guilty	Believing it's your fault
Feeling crazy	Feeling lonely

1. What specifically do you need deliverance from?
2. What physical sickness, afflictions, or disorders do you have, if any?
3. Have you ever been to a psychiatrist or therapist, and were you diagnosed?
4. Are you willing to forgive?
5. Are you willing to forsake sin?
6. Are you willing to be open about your issues and hurts?
7. Have you or your family ever been involved in the occult, witchcraft, the Masons, or with psychics or such?
8. Have you ever been a part of any other religions besides Christianity?
9. Anything else you'd like to mention?

APPENDIX B

SPIRITUAL ASSESSMENT

1. What would you like to accomplish during these sessions?
2. If Jesus was to come back now, where would you go and how do you know?
3. Do you have any sin issue or struggles?
4. Do you speak in tongues? How often?
5. How often do you pray, fast, read your Bible?
6. How often do you attend church?
7. What church do you belong to? Denomination?
8. What churches, religions, groups, or cults have you belonged to? What about your family?
9. What negative beliefs have you had about God?
10. Are you willing to commit to seeking God on a daily basis and being faithful to church?

APPENDIX C

CHECKLIST FOR ADMINISTERING DELIVERANCE

This list is for the team leader to check. This allows the counselor to pick up where they've left off. As the team becomes larger, there should be a director in place who receives and files these forms and holds the teams accountable and provides support. This checklist is a way of tracking the process and seeing where each team is at in the process.

Name:

Email address:

Phone number:

Age:

Goal:

- Removal of sin
- Removing unforgiveness
- Breaking word curses
- Removal of generational sins & curses
- Breaking ungodly soul ties
- Healing trauma & grief
- Deliverance from demons

Results and comments:

APPENDIX D

HOW TO MAINTAIN YOUR FREEDOM

I. Develop a consistent prayer life.

And he spake a parable unto them to this end, that men ought always to pray, and not to faint. ~ Luke 18:1

Praying always with all prayer and supplication in the Spirit, and watching thereunto with all perseverance and supplication for all saints. ~ Ephesians 6:18

II. Read your Bible and live it.

Wherefore laying aside all malice, and all guile, and hypocrisies, and envies, and all evil speakings, As newborn babes, desire the sincere milk of the word, that ye may grow thereby. ~ 1 Peter 2

But he answered and said, It is written, Man shall not live by bread alone, but by every word that proceedeth out of the mouth of God. ~ Matthew 4:4

III.   Cultivate a daily life of praise.

In every thing give thanks: for this is the will of God in Christ Jesus concerning you. ~ 1 Thessalonians 5:18

IV.   Be faithful to a Spirit-filled Bible-believing church.

Not forsaking the assembling of ourselves together, as the manner of some is; but exhorting one another: and so much the more, as ye see the day approaching. ~ Hebrews 10:25

V.   Continue to live a life of forgiveness for yourself and others.

For if ye forgive men their trespasses, your heavenly Father will also forgive you: But if ye forgive not men their trespasses, neither will your Father forgive your trespasses. ~ Matthew 6:14-15

VI.   Actively resist the devil.

Submit yourselves therefore to God. Resist the devil, and he will flee from you. ~ James 4:7

VII. Separate yourself from people, places, and things that will hinder your relationship with God.

Wherefore come out from among them, and be ye separate, saith the

Lord, and touch not the unclean thing; and I will receive you. ~ *2 Corinthians 6:17*

VIII. Stop sinning. If you fall, repent and turn from it immediately.

My little children, these things write I unto you, that ye sin not. And if any man sin, we have an advocate with the Father, Jesus Christ the righteous: And he is the propitiation for our sins: and not for ours only, but also for the sins of the whole world. ~ *1 John 2:1-2*

ABOUT THE AUTHOR

BIOGRAPHY

Timothy G. Lane has been involved in inner healing and deliverance for over ten years. He has a Christian counseling practice called LaneHelps and through his healing and deliverance model has seen people delivered from major depression, anxiety disorders, grief, trauma, and strong demonization, to name a few. Lane has also worked as a secular therapist for over seven years. He has an extensive background in individual and family counseling. He's also worked as a clinical therapist for the Chicago Housing Authority and Chicago Public Schools. Timothy Lane is a third-generation pastor and is a powerful teacher and trainer. He holds a Masters in Counseling, BA in Psychology, and BA in Theology.

75260507R00089

Made in the USA
Columbia, SC
19 September 2019